If The Cup Could Talk

If The
CUP
Could Talk

Michael Ulmer

Sleeping Bear Press

PUBLISHER

Sleeping Bear Press
310 North Main
P.O. Box 20
Chelsea, Michigan 48118
www.sleepingbearpress.com

Printed and bound in Canada
10 9 8 7 6 5 4 3 2 1

Library of Congress Cataloging-in-Publication Data
Ulmer, Michael,
If the cup could talk / by Mike Ulmer.
p. cm.
ISBN 1-886947-62-7
1. Stanley Cup (Hockey) I. Title.
GV847.7.U46 2000
796.962'648--dc21

00-008964

To James Pollock and his Dad.
And to my Uncle Gerry, thanks for the pennants.

Table of Contents

Gravestones in Silver....................................15

The Cup Takes Shape...................................21

Keepers of the Cup......................................29

The Early Days...39

Bad Joe Hall...51

Mistakes, They Made a Few 53

Lindsay's Greatest Pass...............................57

The Snub..65

Bashin' Bill 67

At Home with Henri....................................73

The Golden Book 77

Mutual Friends...81

A Hero Named Wally..................................87

Silver and Gold 93

One Final Spring 97

Who's the Round Guy with Al? 103

The Manhattan Transfer 105

Stanley C. Riley...109

The Heaviest Trophy...................................113

The Cup before becoming the "Elephant Leg." (Hockey Hall of Fame Archives)

Prologue

SILENCE IS SILVER

Let us say this from the beginning: the Stanley Cup can't talk, speech being one of the few miracles it has not yet wrought. Forged in silver, the Cup, alas, is not silver-tongued. The only words ascribed to the Stanley Cup are the names it bears. But in those names, and in the stories behind them, is the power to evoke and inspire, chasten and intimidate. Those names lift the Stanley Cup above the field. It has no equal in sports; no trophy past, present, or future, can match its bearing and its dignity.

Consider that stature for a moment. While hockey is the only game of consequence in Canada, in the United States hockey's appeal lags behind football, basketball, baseball, and, in much of the country, college athletics. And yet, the appeal of the Cup, a bauble initiated as a goodwill gesture more than 100 years ago, laps the field. If presented with a picture of the Stanley Cup, more North American fans could name it than could identify the Vince Lombardi Trophy, emblematic of NFL supremacy, or the Larry O'Brien Trophy, bestowed upon the NBA champion, or Major League Baseball's pennant-festooned championship trophy. In size and stature, it towers over the rest, a man among boys.

There is an immense dignity in the Stanley Cup. No matter what the hijinks, and surely it has proved itself a remarkably good sport, the Cup's charisma only heightens with time. The famous are awestruck by its celebrity. Ballplayers such as the New York Mets' Mike Piazza, a hockey fan from Philadelphia, and the Braves' Tom Glavine, a Boston Bruins' draft choice, beg photographers to snap a picture of them with the Cup. Everyday people timidly

9

reach out to touch it, and then look for their reflection in the polished silver.

They not only see themselves, they see the names of all who claimed the Cup rapped in by a Montreal woman named Louise St. Jacques and before St. Jacques, her mentor, Doug Boffey and before them, Arno and Paul Petersen. Only those four have brandished an engraver's hammer and stamps against the Cup since the Second World War.

When you reach hockey's Mount Olympus, they hammer your name in letters 1/32nd of an inch deep, and if a glance at the Stanley Cup is a celebration of the names it bears, it is also a mute requiem for those such as Buffalo Sabre great Gilbert Perreault and longtime Ranger stars Harry Howell and Mike Gartner, whose excellence couldn't overcome circumstance. "You'd love to have won it," Gartner has often said, "but it's a question of being in the right situation. A lot of great players haven't won it."

True enough. Champions still, they contribute to the Cups' unique charisma by their absence. Implicit in the message of the names engraved into the Cup is the greatness of those who will never be; the grandest of jewels can be seen by all, but worn only by a select few.

"We sweated every day of the year to win the Stanley Cup and I never obtained it," said Emile Francis, longtime coach of the New York Rangers, executive of the Rangers, St. Louis Blues, and Hartford Whalers and a member of the Hockey Hall of Fame. "If I said it didn't hurt, I would be lying. Because it does."

So pristine is the Stanley Cup's image, it has been the font used for at least one christening. Colorado Avalanche defenseman Sylvain Lefebvre christened one of his children in the Cup when the Avs took home the trophy in 1996.

An Ontario woman named Cheryl Riley found magic in it, a miracle baby named Stanley conceived after she kissed the Cup.

Despite its abundant mythology, the Stanley Cup-mined, minted, crafted, and awarded by men—is imbued as much with error as excellence. There are three teams on the Cup who shouldn't be there, and numerous misspellings. The original bowl has been the subject of several lifetimes of abuse. It has been kicked onto a frozen canal, used as a flowerpot, and left on a curb in an early morning revelry. Hundreds of people, some players, mostly anonymous vandals, have taken a nail and scratched their names into the silver. Even the men who stole it could not resist leaving their names.

So many stories have been rubbed like polish into that Cup that it stands as a piece of organic art. It is as alive as the people who covet and grasp it, each new tale or adventure just adds to the burnish. One year, a Montreal club, believed to be the Wanderers, left the Cup at the home of a photographer. The Cup was forgotten and the photographer's mother commandeered it, filled it with earth and planted geraniums in it for a display in the front window of her son's business.

In 1910, with the Montreal Wanderers in possession of the Cup, one of the players, the owner of a bowling alley, saw a chance to use the Cup for promotional purposes. He filled it with gum and sold it from the Cup.

Sometimes, the Cup's absence has been carefully planned. In 1947, the Leafs beat the Canadiens in six games to claim the title, but there was no Cup to present. Toronto owner Conn Smythe didn't want to move the Cup from Montreal, where it was displayed in a store, because he believed sportswriters would learn of the move and interpret it as overconfidence by his players. Two weeks after it was won, the Cup was transferred to Toronto.

There are now, in fact, three Stanley Cups. The original bowl and bands are retired and sealed in shatterproof Plexiglas, protected by alarms at the Hockey Hall of Fame. The presentation Cup, created in time for the 1962 season and brandished by the captain from every team since then, and a replica Cup, which never leaves the Hockey Hall of Fame but stands in for the presentation Cup when it is on the road or with players from the winning team.

The Stanley Cup may be the only object in the world that combines immense dignity and history with a design that forces you to carry it as you would a keg of beer. You hold the Stanley Cup by the base and by the bowl. Somehow it looks best when it is suspended horizontally in the air and shaken. It is as rough as the men who fight for it.

"It is like the trophy that is brought back from the hunt," said six-time winner Ken Dryden. "You just watch the way people look at it, the way they handle it, the way they pass it. They don't hold it down low; they hold it above their heads. They hold it in that sense of triumph."

It is, in fact, built like a person, with a stout belly, a long neck, and a bowl for a head and it is treated as such. While always buffed and gleaming, the Stanley Cup, like a favorite worldly uncle, wears its miles and its scars, like the 16 capital Xs ordered by the NHL when it was learned the name of Basil Pocklington, father of former Edmonton Oilers' owner Peter Pocklington, had been inscribed. There is no subterfuge about it. Like the lines on an old man's face, the Cup's history is evident at a glance. Just read the names and feel its oft-dented contours.

That the Stanley Cup cannot talk is good and just. It would never undermine its own stature with tales of the indignities it has endured. Red Kelly's baby boy Conn is one the many undi-apered babies who has sullied its silver. Ed Olczyk, a winner with the Rangers, let a horse eat oats from its bowl in 1994. Discretion would not allow it to discuss the afternoon it spent with Chris Simon on a quiet Northern Ontario Lake with his father, or in a quiet room where Denis Potvin and his gravely ill father sat. It has seen as much sadness as any mortal man, but for generations of hockey players the Stanley Cup remains the perfect confidant.

This is not to describe the Cup as undemanding. Winning it is the toughest two months a professional athlete will endure. "Maybe that's why," said Dallas Star gunner Mike Modano, "people break down when they finally get it. It takes so much out of you just to get the chance to hold it."

And then it gives back, over the one or two days every player has the use of it and then, over the rest of the player's lifetime. In hockey, immortality is buried in silver 1/32nd of an inch deep.

In these pages, the players who won the Stanley Cup, the white-gloved men who carry it, the people whose lives were altered by it, can render their tributes and give voice to their gratitude. It is a homage carried in word and tone by many voices. No, the Cup can't talk, but it's time someone spoke for Stanley. Here are the stories his friends would tell; the stories, they feel, he would tell himself.

Mike Ulmer
Hamilton, Ontario
Dec 12, 1999

Dallas Stars' Guy Carbonneau in victory parade, 1999.
(Phil Pritchard / Hockey Hall of Fame Archives)

The original Cup, scratches and all. (Hockey Hall of Fame Archives)

Chapter 1

GRAVESTONES IN SILVER

They left their marks with nails or knives. A few even used engraving equipment. They did it in quiet moments and at raucous parties. They did it alone, as old men and children, as famous men and men-next-door. Whatever the means, whatever the number of witnesses or the circumstance, the motive was the same: to leave a mark, a private little secret on a pleasant little trophy that would later become an immensely public sporting talisman.

Now, their names serve as a sort of hockey graveyard where the famous and those known to only a few live on, studied for a few seconds by thousands a day milling in the vault of the Bell Great Hall of the Hockey Hall of Fame in Toronto. They are gravestones etched into silver.

The original bowl, the one commissioned by the Earl of Stanley and bearing his insignia, has been ensconced in Plexiglas since it was brought to Toronto in 1969. Tourists and hockey fans must strain to see the names scratched onto the bowl. Most notice Cyclone Taylor's 'Fred W Taylor' but, tired of the eyestrain and craning their neck, they lose interest.

Only by removing the bowl from its Plexiglas case does the mystery take flight. There are hundreds, perhaps thousands, of names scratched into the bowl, inside the fluting, alongside the ring, on any surface that could accommodate a few letters. With the passing of time, insignias have become enigmas. There is a name of a mascot on the bowl, not far from the scrawl 'Hall of Famer Sprague Cleghorn,' perhaps an eighth of an inch high. It reads:

"Bow Wow." The best guess of the cryptic meaning lies with the Quebec Bulldogs, Cup winners in 1912 and 1913 as members of the NHL forerunner, the National Hockey Association. The Bulldogs' mutt mascot was prominently displayed in the 1913 championship photo but there is no adjacent autograph to identify a Bulldogs' member in the same script. The Bulldogs, the pride of the provincial capital, Quebec City, featured stars such as Phantom Joe Malone and Paddy Moran but the franchise shifted to Hamilton in 1920.

In tiny script under the bowl, a man named R.T. Garner has inscribed his name and then, under it, "long lives Canadiens." While the layers of names and words are nearly impossible to itemize, the Canadiens' reference seems to be the only unofficial team reference scratched into the Cup.

Percy LeSueur, the Stanley Cup's original ringer, chipped in his name. LeSueur, a onetime bankteller and a stand-up goalie from Smiths Falls, near Ottawa, helped the Ottawa Silver Seven very nearly overcome a 9-1 deficit in a two-goal, total goals series with Montreal in 1906. LeSueur was inserted into the second game as the Silver seven rallied but eventually lost on a goal by future New York Rangers' General Manager Lester Patrick. For his trouble, LeSueur was paid $100 but the original bowl will always bear his scratched-in name. He would later be credited with inventing the gauntlet goal glove and the goal net the NHL used from 1912 to 1925. Still later he would serve as the coach of the NHL's Hamilton Tigers and the house manager of the Detroit Olympia.

To the shiny bowl they all came, the famous and the anonymous. Rangers' star Bun Cook scratched his name on the Cup in at least three spots. In 1995, he would be posthumously enshrined in the Hockey Hall of Fame.

Hamilton (Hamby) Shore scrawled his name on the outside of the bowl in 1911 while a member of the National Hockey Association's Ottawa Senators. Seven years later, he would be killed in the influenza epidemic.

Nearby, separated by a couple of inches, are the Cleghorn broth-

The Quebec Bulldogs, 1912-1913. Did they put "bow wow"
on the Cup? (Hockey Hall of Fame Archives)

ers. Sprague Cleghorn played for 17 seasons as a star rushing
defenseman in the NHA and NHL and stood as the game's premier master of roughhouse. He is believed to have scratched
his name on the Cup in 1924, not far from the signature of his
slick goal-scoring brother, Odie. The brothers were members of
the Montreal Canadiens and involved in one of the most famous
Cup incidents when, in 1924, still flush from their Stanley Cup
win, they stopped to change a flat tire en route to the home of
Canadiens' manager Leo Dandurand. Somehow, the Cup was left
on a Montreal street corner during the repair and overlooked. The
men, no doubt in fine spirits, drove away and it wasn't until
much later in the evening that someone realized the Cup had
been left behind. The players returned to the corner and found
the Stanley Cup exactly where they had left it.

Odie would work as a league referee. One night he worked a
game involving the New York Americans and New York Rangers,

which had been the subject of heavy betting by members of the New York organized crime syndicate. Late in the scoreless game, Americans' defenseman Hoe Simpson threw his stick at the puck to prevent a breakaway. The rules of the time called for an automatic goal, which Cleghorn awarded to the Rangers. The game ended 1-0 and the gamblers rioted in an attempt to reach Cleghorn. Riot police with drawn guns had to escort him back to his hotel.

The Cleghorns would not long be parted by death. Sprague Cleghorn was hit by a car on the way to work and died in Ottawa at the age of 65 in 1956. The day he was to attend his brother's funeral, they found Odie, 66, dead in his bed of a heart attack.

Inside the bowl, seven members of the Toronto Blue Shirts have scratched their names, including coach Frank Carroll. Hall of Famer Marty Walsh chipped in his name in 1909. Two years later he would score ten goals in a game. Exactly when Harry Cameron scratched in his name will never be known. Cameron is the only man to have played with three Toronto Stanley Cup winners, the Blue Shirts in 1914, the Arenas in 1918, and the St. Pats in 1921-22.

Harold (Punch) Broadbent scratched his name into the Cup as a member of the Ottawa Senators, either in the early 1920s or with the Montreal Maroons in 1926. Broadbent still owns the record for consecutive games with a goal, 16. He was nominated to the Hall of Fame in 1962.

Jack Walker, another signee, was the greatest defensive forward of his time. He was known as the father of the "sweep" or "poke" check. Walker helped bring the first Stanley Cup to American soil with the Seattle Metropolitans in 1917, forever killing any notion of hockey remaining a Canadian monopoly.

The most startling signature belongs to Art Ross, who may have scratched his name onto the Cup in 1907. Ross was paid $2,000 for a two-game stint with the Kenora Thistles that landed them the Cup that year. The following season, he won another Cup, this time with the Montreal Wanderers. Even while under the employ of the Wanderers, he was often paid to show up and

Doug MacLellan (Hockey Hall of Fame Archives)

Even under the watchful eyes of the Royal Canadian Mounted Police, the Cup
has crossed borders and visited Washington D.C. on a number of occasions.
(Canadian Embassy / Hockey Hall of Fame Archives)

19

play for other teams during important games.

Ross would find a higher stardom as a manager. Hired in 1924 as the original coach and general manager for the Boston Bruins, Ross's team would win 10 division titles and three Stanley Cups. While the Art Ross Trophy, designated to the leading scorer for each season, bears his name, he scored just one goal in three NHL games but it was his final design of the puck that would remain to this day. The Art Ross net, with its deep and padded wells, all but eliminated disputes about whether a goal had been scored by trapping the puck. It was in use until 1984.

Two boys scratched their names into the Cup with a nail in the late 1920s, and then would grow to see their names officially inscribed. Lynn and Muzz Patrick found the Cup in a cardboard box in the basement of their home in Victoria, British Columbia. The boys' father, Lester Patrick was the coach and general manager of the 1928 Cup champs Victoria Cougars. The boys would have their names engraved for real as members of the 1940 Cup-winning New York Rangers.

Chapter 2

THE CUP TAKES SHAPE

By the mid-1940s, the Cup was becoming ungainly. It was 18 rings high and the trophy towered above any player who lifted it. The trophy had been nicknamed the Elephant Leg and looked like nothing more than a thick silverplated pipe with a bowl on top.

The NHL's head office was then in Montreal and in 1948, the league chose Montreal silversmith C.P. 'Carl' Petersen for the job of redesigning the trophy. Although only 34, Petersen was already a master artisan when he emigrated from Denmark 19 years before.

Denmark in the 1920s was renowned for its rich art world that prominently included work in silver. Petersen had been a sculptor and art teacher in Copenhagen. The Danish style stressed streamlined elements, with ornamentation serving to set off that form. Those were sensibilities that Petersen would eventually perfectly imbue into the Stanley Cup.

After the war, Petersen's studio thrived and he ran it with his three sons, Arno, who would succeed him as the official Cup engraver, John Paul, and Ole. The Stanley Cup was a small element of Petersen's business. The quality of his silver jewelry, table services and repair and restorative work was known across North America. By the time he was asked to work on the Stanley Cup, his firm was importing four tons of silver yearly and employing 20 silversmiths at its Montreal studio.

Petersen fashioned new bands into which the names were stamped. The renovation meant names were placed closer together

The Cup in its "Elephant Leg" stage.
(Hockey Hall of Fame Archives)

to gain more room. Inappropriate names were removed and the frame of the trophy was done in hollow aluminum. The interior of the trophy had been wood and the change dropped the weight of the trophy from 50 pounds to its current 32. The bowl and collar were made to be removable as well, making it easier to pass between players and-not incidentally-to drink from.

Petersen contented himself with applying new names to the Cup every summer, but by the mid-1960s, there was another problem. League officials were in full fret over the original bowl. Because its silver-alloy combination would become brittle over

Carl Petersen, Danish designer of the current Stanley Cup.
(Hockey Hall of Fame Archives)

time, a fear was developing at the head office that if dropped, the Stanley Cup could shatter like a piece of china.

"Because it was subject to being destroyed if it was kicked around too much—which it was" explained longtime NHL executive vice-president Bryan O'Neill, "it was decided to take that bowl off and put it on permanent display at the Hall of Fame and to do a replica in sterling, matching every scratch, each name, absolutely perfectly."

At 72, Petersen was again entrusted with the job and his work was so detailed, he even included some of the bite marks left

23

by players on the original bowl. The bowl was removed from the Cup in 1967 and the plan to keep the original in the Hall of Fame was forgotten. The original bowl sat on Petersen's desk for three years before, in the wake of the theft of his replica, he brought the original bowl to Toronto and plunked it on the desk of Hall of Fame curator Lefty Reid. Petersen's replica has existed as the Stanley Cup ever since.

The Cup was damaged during Stanley Cup celebrations in 1992 and 1993. Petersen's successor Doug Boffey added another dusting of silver to the neck and reinforced the neck from the inside. Externally, it has remained unmodified, save for 1991 when the Pittsburgh Penguins filled the last space on the fifth and bottom band, mandating the retirement of Petersen's first band.

Petersen died in 1977 and C.P. Petersen and Sons, buffeted by skyrocketing silver prices and consumer buying changes, closed in 1979. Still, 20 years after his death and five decades after his original commission, the elements of Carl Petersen's training, streamlined form offset by decorative elements, retain their hold in his greatest work.

That work is now entrusted to 41-year-old Louise St. Jacques, the first female to enter the names on the Stanley Cup. St. Jacques is a mother of one, except for a week or two in late summer when her charge doubles to include not only five-year-old Eric, but also Stanley, her annual summer boarder.

Every August or September, the presentation cup and the spare kept at the Toronto's Hockey Hall of Fame are entrusted to St. Jacques for 10 days of care and engraving.

She is the restorer of its luster, the steady maternal hand that refurbishes the sports world's most masculine trophy. For those 10 days, he is hers. "I am," she says with an artisan's pride, "the only person who sees it every year."

She meets it at the airport in Montreal, where, inevitably, word of its arrival prompts a crowd wanting a look. St. Jacques generally acquiesces before driving it to the Montreal office she shares with longtime Cup engraver and mentor Doug Boffey.

Then come the most pressure-filled days of her year. St. Jacques

Louise St. Jacques, current engraver for the Cup, returns rings to
the base after polishing. (Doug Boffey / Hockey Hall of Fame Archives)

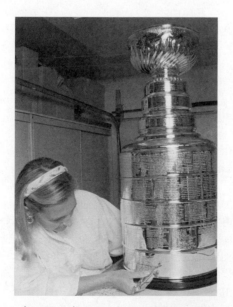

Jacques takes measurements to ensure
accurate spacing of names on the Cup.
(Doug Boffey / Hockey Hall of Fame Archives)

carefully disassembles the trophy with custom-made tools, separating the bowl, the neck, and the five name-bearing rings. The sterling silver Cup is hollow, but a plastic plate has been installed at the bottom to keep people from scratching their initials inside. The five rings are slid off the base and dipped in solvent to remove the protective lacquer. The Cup is then relacquered and buffed. Since drinking champagne, beer, and virtually every other liquid is part of the Cup tradition, the bowl is the only part of the trophy that is not lacquered.

The bands are individually clamped onto a homemade circular jig that serves as a steel background for the stamping. Special hammers with different head weights are used to hammer the punch. A steel edge is used to keep the punch line straight.

Polishing is a problem. If the Cup is roughed or rubbed too often, the metal starts to disappear and the names become less legible, so the Cup undergoes a deep polish only once every four or five years. St. Jacques uses a small hammer and "gravers" (stamps) bearing upper- or lowercase letters to inscribe each name supplied by the NHL. Sliding guides are used to put the letters more or less in alignment, but the skill of the engraver is evident to a practiced eye.

Thanks to 20 years of engraving experience, she navigates about the Cup smoothly. St. Jacques is still young enough that the twin curses of her craft, failing eyes and nervous hands, have not yet afflicted her. Still, she works in only 90-minute bursts before pausing to rest. Each name takes about half an hour to inscribe. "It's very stressful," St. Jacques said. "You don't want to make a mistake. I go over and over the list; every letter you punch in, you look at the paper again. You check and check."

St. Jacques has worked for Boffey since 1978, when she heard about his business and applied on a whim. She honed her skills engraving jewelry and other trophies, but did not raise a hammer to the Cup until her tenth year of the job. The process is virtually unchanged since Carl Petersen originated it and the engravers have a tradition of their own. Upon an engraver's retirement from the Cup, the new engraver stamps the old one's initials inside the Cup.

Even now, a decade into her duties, St. Jacques remains unjaundiced over the Cup's appeal. "There has never been a bad word said about it," she said. "No one criticizes the Stanley Cup. When you see it, it's a beautiful trophy. You can't help but stare at it. When we polish it up at the end, God, it looks nice."

One of many Cup "keepers," Paul Oke (Mark Hicks)

Chapter 3

KEEPERS OF THE CUP

They elicit tumultuous cheers wherever they go, yet no one quite remembers what they look like. In the spotlight, yet still somehow in the shadows, they are the current handlers of the Stanley Cup, the possessors of dream jobs, the men in the white gloves.

Four men: Phil Pritchard, Craig Campbell, Walter Neubrand and Paul Oke are the custodians of the Stanley Cup, or what is — inside the Hockey Hall of Fame—known as the Presentation Cup.

The original bowl commissioned by Lord Stanley resides in the Hall, ensconced in a Plexiglas display case. The original bands are also sealed and available for public viewing, and never leave the Hockey Hall of Fame.

Whenever it is available, the Presentation Cup, the one hoisted by winning captains every year and passed around between teammates and friends, is also on display at the Hall. Because the Cup has a full itinerary of events year-round, a replica Cup is used at the Hall when the Presentation Cup is on the road. The replica is identical to the Presentation Cup in all but the tiniest of details. Basil Pocklington's name, X'd out on the Presentation Cup, is omitted altogether from the replica. Because the silver alloy of the Presentation Cup could not be reproduced, the replica Cup is about four pounds heavier than the Presentation Cup.

What is the annual highlight for Cup watchers has only evolved as a television moment over the last generation. The presentation of the Cup, the most evocative moment of any final, was treated as an afterthought through the NHL's first half-century.

Since radio was the NHL's first electronic medium, most people had only seen newspaper pictures of the Cup. Even after the introduction of television, producers treated the presentation of the Cup as an afterthought to the game. NHL security people would put it on a card table, and it would be pushed beside the league president during a commercial break. After a short speech, the president bestowed the Cup on the winning captain and it disappeared from public view. Any televised depiction of the Cup is either the Presentation Cup, or in the case of Cups used in television commercials for Federal Express and Labatt's Blue beer, one of a couple of league-sanctioned copies. One copy, originally used in the Canadian hockey television movie *Net Worth*, is trotted out for Hockey Night in Canada's set design every spring during the Stanley Cup play-offs.

What has become a staple of Cup night, the sight of the Cup being carried by Hall of Fame employees wearing the blue Hall of Fame blazers and, of course, the white gloves, didn't begin until 1994. The white gloves evolved under the auspices of commissioner Gary Bettman, when the League began considering how to more prominently feature the presentation of the Cup. "We wanted to show the Cup being presented," said Pritchard, the Hall's director of information and acquisitions, "the way it should be. The white gloves really speak to what it is."

The gloves are standard equipment when dealing with artifacts. "Every museum uses these," Pritchard said. "They're usually behind the scenes because you don't want the acid from your fingers to get onto the artifacts. This is one of the prime artifacts in the world, let alone in the hockey world, so it's natural that you would wear white gloves with it." The ritual handing over of the Cup includes a personal ritual for Pritchard. He uses the same set of gloves every year. Whether presenting the Stanley Cup in the middle of a wildly cheering arena or bringing it to a player's coffee table, the Stanley Cup attendant always wears white gloves.

If a team wins the Stanley Cup on the road, Pritchard and Campbell are there in the winning city with the Cup. If the Cup

The Stanley Cup—"Ticket for Montreal, please."
Railway Ticket Agent—"Return?"
The Stanley Cup—"No; I'm not coming back."

(Hockey Hall of Fame Archives)

is won at home, they begin the process of chaperoning it immediately.

The hijinks usually begin before midnight. The postgame party
in the dressing room doesn't break up until two or three a.m.
A private party is usually next, where the winners toast themselves until dawn.

And then the tour begins.

In the Cup's first half-century, players were usually estranged
from the trophy not long after winning it. The Cup was presented, handed back to the league, and locked up for another year.
"The game started at 8:30 and it would end around 10:40,"

remembered Red Wings' Hall of Famer Ted Lindsay. "By the time we got showered, it would be midnight and we wouldn't have eaten since earlier in the day so there would be a meal and a party at a hotel. Today they have a parade. Back then the parade was the players driving home. That was it. You were lucky if you saw the Cup again the next year."

"Through the 1970s and 1980s, the team got it for a couple of weeks," Pritchard said. "It would be in Edmonton, at Wayne Gretzky's or Mark Messier's house for a week or so. When the Penguins got it, Lemieux would have gotten it, Jagr would have gotten it, but not every player got it."

The idea of booking and brokering time for players and coaches to enjoy the Cup, properly escorted by a Cup chaperone, didn't begin until the New Jersey Devils won the Cup. It was a brilliant idea, but as natural as it seems now, some viewed it as heretical.

So deep was the Montreal Canadians' regard for the Cup, the idea of possessing the Cup and taking it home would have been seen as ludicrous. "We never would have had the Stanley Cup to take home," said Toronto Maple Leafs' president Ken Dryden, a six-time Cup winner. "There was the story of Guy Lafleur taking it home and putting it on the front lawn in Thurso. But that was Guy Lafleur. He was the star. But taking it home, boy, what gall!"

Lafleur did in fact once rise up from a team party and without a word of explanation, put the cup in the trunk of his car and drove to his parents' home in Thurso. It stayed there for a day. "I figured the team would be wondering where it was, so I brought it back," Lafleur said. When New Jersey Devil Stephane Richer brought the Cup to the area in 1995, he was taken aback by the legacy of Lafleur's visit. "People fifty-five and sixty years old came up to me with pictures they had taken with Lafleur 20 years ago," Richer said. "That started to freak me out. That's when I realized how lucky I was."

The Cup's sojourn in Edmonton, first in 1984 and then 1985, 1987, 1988, and 1990, included riotous tours of bars, restau-

The Cup visits Sweden. (Walter Neubrand / Hockey Hall of Fame Archives)

rants, and parties. It marked the first time that fans in the winning city could see and touch the Cup up close. "In Edmonton, so many people had a chance to touch it and drink from it," longtime Oilers' star Mark Messier said. "A lot of people who had only seen it on TV had an opportunity to get up close and take a picture. Just seeing the people's reactions to that was worth it." The players got to celebrate through the summer with the Cup, but there was one problem. As a result of being passed through so many hands, the Cup was taking a terrible beating.

While distributing the Cup was an excellent idea, it needed a chaperone. "The players now know that when they have the Cup, someone from the Hall always comes with it," Pritchard said. He has occasionally chaperoned the Cup and he remains amazed at its appeal. "When Colorado won it, (Avalanche goalie) Patrick Roy was in a celebrity golf tournament in Lake Tahoe. He wanted the Cup there, so we brought it to him. There were all these sports stars and celebrities everywhere, but the Cup had the biggest lineup of people wanting to see it."

Pritchard was in Washington doing some PR work in the spring of 1998 and was standing with the Cup on a busy corner on Pennsylvania Avenue. A tour bus filled with children stopped abruptly in front of him, clogging the intersection. "That's the Cup!" yelled a beefy driver. Pritchard admitted that it was and the driver began relaying information via his microphone to the students. Before Pritchard knew it, he was aboard the bus, walking the Cup through the row of starry-eyed children.

Detroit Red Wing Brendan Shanahan rented a bus and took the Cup on a rolling tour of his hometown of Mimico, Ontario. Later, he would take it by himself and set it next to his father's grave.

Current Cup keeper Walter Neubrand began traveling with the Cup in 1997. He remembers the zeal of Darren McCarty of the Red Wings in bringing the Cup to anyone who wanted to see it. "We were just barnstorming through everywhere and Darren kept saying, 'We've got to get it to the people, we've got to get it to the people.' That was really important to him. I remember one day, we took it to a friend's place in Leamington (Ontario), a little ways from the border. It was a tomato farm and to get to where his friends were, you had to walk through this tomato field. This little shack in the back was filled with McCarty's friends. They had a pool table and a band playing. I remember walking through this great big tomato field, holding the Stanley Cup, saying to myself, what are we doing here? When we finally got there, he put the Stanley Cup right on the pool table, picked up a guitar and started jamming."

"We also took it to a nightspot in Detroit. It was 11 o'clock on a Friday night and the place was just packed. As McCarty reached the door, he turns to me and says 'Walt, are you ready for this?' He walks in and everybody goes wild. There was this huge crowd and he kept getting further and further away. I tried to keep up; I could see the Cup over his head. Then I thought, 'Ah, he can take care of it.'"

Forward Martin Lapointe brought the Cup to his hockey school in Montreal. Assistant coach Dave Lewis tooled around Detroit in his red Viper, his son Ryan next to him, belted in with the Stanley Cup. Yzerman showered with the Cup when he first won it in 1997 and later strapped it to the back of his jet ski and displayed it around a Michigan lake. In Peterborough, Ontario, defenseman Larry Murphy staged a badminton tournament where the losers had to pose with a wooden toilet seat. The winners had their pictures taken with the Cup.

The Cup's effect often seems to transport hockey players back to their childhood when their parents would tuck them in and find them wearing their favorite piece of equipment. Stanley Cup winners often ask if they can sleep with the Cup. "It depends on their behavior during the day," Neubrand said. "If they are responsible with it, we generally say yes. We're usually staying over at the player's place anyway."

Even the men who have retired their white gloves say the Cup had a profound impact on their personal and professional lives.

Scott North is thirty-two years old, with a Rolodex that would make any hockey fan pant.

Need Bobby Hull for your corporate banquet? Is there any chance of landing Gordie Howe for your sports celebrity dinner? Call Scott North, booking agent for the stars. There is only one hockey celebrity for whom Scott North reserves awe: Stanley.

North lives in an expansive house in Burlington, Ontario, near Toronto. He spent eight years at the Hockey Hall of Fame in the early to mid-1990s, much of that time escorting the Stanley Cup to special events. He misses the job and liked the people but there is a Cup-sized hole in his life he has never quite filled.

"The one thing I miss most is the Cup," North said. "Obviously, for selfish reasons, for being able to go to the Stanley Cup finals and those types of events but also, I miss seeing what that inanimate object does for people. I reflect now on what the Stanley Cup did for me. That's what makes him Stanley for me. If he were a person, he would be a very, very close friend because of the chances he gave me. Internally, at the Hall of Fame, he is like a person."

Somehow, the Stanley Cup has become imbued with a character all its own. When it is out of sight, its keepers ask, "Where's Stanley?" or "Have you seen Stan?"

"He's the perfect inanimate object," North said. "He sees things that he will never, ever tell. Your best friend in the world, you might come to a point where discretion might slip a bit. Stanley never tells. He's strong, in control, and very solid."

It happened to North dozens of times. He would be between commitments, pressed for time because invariably, the Cup had been bidden a reluctant and tardy goodbye at the previous destination. When you travel with the Cup, "You are always trying to overextend one event and then having to push it to get to the next one." North said. " I had the attitude that it didn't matter, because Stanley would take care of me. And he did." North replays the typical conversation when, running late, he is pulled over:

Police:" Do you know how fast you were going?"

North: "Officer, I'm sorry but we're going to this event and we've got the Stanley Cup."

Police: "Really? Can I see it?"

North: "Sure, but we've got to do it quick because we've got to get it there."

Police: "Don't worry. I'll escort you."

It offends the keepers of the Cup when it is treated with disrespect. North remembers the Cup returning from Pittsburgh in 1991 and 1992 and Montreal in 1993, rusted from trips into players' swimming pools.

The Cup, North said, supersedes all questions of protocol and procedures. In the fourth game of the 1992 finals, he was detained in the bowels of the Met in Minnesota. "We didn't have any kind of credentials or anything like that and we've got Stanley in the back seat and we've got to get him into the arena. This guy wasn't going to let us in. I said 'It's unfortunate that they didn't get us credentials, but if you want to be responsible for not having the Stanley Cup there, that's fine, we'll just turn around.' Whoosh, we were in."

North and the others who have kept the Cup found their friend more than willing to let them bask in his celebrity status. Toronto resident Rob Kardas remembers his travels with Stanley. Kardas accompanied the Cup with the Detroit Red Wings in the summer of 1997. He checked the Cup as baggage in Detroit and then, a few moments later, was paged to the Northwest Airlines ticket counter. "When I got there, they said, 'Is this the Stanley Cup?' I said 'Yes.' They begged me to take it out of the case so they could get their picture taken with it. I did, and there were about 30 of them in the picture. Then they upgraded me to first class. I was on Jay Leno for about a second," recalled Kardas. "They gave Stanley his own dressing room and I got to use it too. Jay Leno came down and asked me about it. (Actor) Paul Reiser was a guest on the show that night and he and I talked about it for a long time."

Sometimes, Kardas found himself with different types of heroes. "I was with (Red Wings' defenseman) Aaron Ward when he took it to a Children's Cancer hospital in Ann Arbor. It was unbelievable to see those kids and the way they reacted to Stanley. I really believe it's immeasurable, how many more seconds, minutes, and hours, he gave those children."

Jeff Graham, another one-time Cup handler who broke-in working with the Wings, remembers Red Wings tough guy Darren McCarty taking the Cup to visit different kinds of bad boys. "We were playing a charity game in Michigan and the police asked Darren if he would come to police headquarters with the Cup. He said he would and when he was there, they asked him if he wanted to have a look in the holding cell. He said sure, and we walked through these holding cells. There must have been 70 or 80 guys there with Darren McCarty and the Stanley Cup.

These guys were hockey fans and they asked him for his autograph. He said they were in here for a reason, and he would be glad to give them autographs...after they got out of jail."

When he started transporting the Cup, Graham was so fearful of losing it he refused to leave it in the car while he ate in a restaurant. "I was taking it to Brendan Shanahan in Toronto and I stopped not far from Toronto at a Swiss Chalet. The waitress wouldn't let me put the case in the restaurant-there was no room. Finally, she said I could eat where the staff eats in the back. About 10 minutes later she came back and said, 'I have to know what's in the box.' I told her it was the Stanley Cup. She asked if I would mind if the staff took a picture with it. I said that would be fine, after I finished. What I didn't know is that she told someone, who told someone else, who told someone else. All of a sudden, about half the people in the restaurant get up, go to their cars and get their cameras. They took about 30 photos before I could get it out of that restaurant."

Graham had his own little tradition. When making an overnight stay, he would wheel the Cup case into his room, hoist Stanley out and position it on top of the case.

"That way," he said, "when I woke up, I would look to the foot of the bed. Stanley would be the first thing I would see."

Chapter 4

THE EARLY DAYS

The most established, most venerable trophy in professional sports began as something as intangible as a few good intentions stacked seven and a half inches tall.

Its patron was Lord Stanley of Preston, the Sixth Stanley of Preston, sixth in the viceregal line. His full title was representative of his lofty peerage: "Right Honorable Sir Frederick Arthur Stanley, Baron Stanley of Preston, in the County of Lancaster, in the Peerage of Great Britain, Knight Grand Cross of the Most Honorable Order of Bath."

When he arrived as the British royalty's representative to its commonwealth of Canada in 1888, Lord Stanley was famous as an English sportsman with a particular fondness for horse racing, cricket, and football (soccer). Hockey, while still primitive, was enjoying explosive growth, and he took to the sport almost as soon as he arrived.

Hockey's roots have been traced to eighteenth century England, Ireland, and Scotland. The game was refined slightly in Canada in the late 1800s. A handful of students from McGill University in Montreal formalized the rules. Rather than a ball, they agreed on a piece of rubber that was named a puck. Teams were limited to nine a side. Up until 1899, goals were just two uprights with no nets or even a bar across the top. Forward passes were outlawed and on-ice umpires stood on the ice and waved a flag if they thought the puck had entered the goal. There was no standard term for a penalty; the umpires decided the time off a player would be assessed at the moment of infraction.

Still, the game featured the rudiments of what was to come, skill and speed. Most importantly, it gave sportsmen, idled by winter's hold, something to do when the weather turned cold. The first organized league was founded in Kingston in 1886 and the game swept across Ontario.

Lord Stanley liked hockey the first time he saw the game and followed the local Ottawa City squad, the home team of the Canadian capital to which he was posted. He sponsored the creation of a large outdoor rink on the ample grounds of his residence and gave his blessing to the formation of a Government House hockey team.

The Rideau Rebels were a collection of upper-class boys and members of the officer corps stationed in Ottawa. Two of his sons, Algernon and Arthur, played on the team and craving a challenge, the Rebels began to arrange games. The boys challenged Ottawa City to a match and were handily defeated, but the excitement around that challenge stayed with Lord Stanley and would be the earliest genesis of the Stanley Cup play-offs.

Pressure began to build for a trophy, both from the Stanley boys and from Lord Kilcoursie, a trusted aide to Stanley and a forward on the Rebels. It would give the Rebels, as well as Ottawa City and other teams, something for which to compete.

Lord Stanley commissioned a championship bowl from the finest silversmiths in London and while he was not enamored of the price-the bowl cost the equivalent of $48-the trophy was created and delivered nonetheless. The bowl was fashioned from a silver and nickel alloy. It measured 7 1/2 inches deep and 11 1/2 inches across. It sat on an ebony base.

In March 1892, at a banquet given for the Ottawa Club, Lord Kilcoursie read a letter from Lord Stanley. The letter formalized Lord Stanley's intention to create a trophy worthy of challenge and set up the framework so the best teams in the country could vie for his donated bit of silverware. The letter stated:

I have for some time been thinking it would be a good thing if there were a challenge cup, which could be held from year to

Lord Stanley, "Right Honorable Sir Frederick Arthur Stanley,
Baron Stanley of Preston." (Hockey Hall of Fame Archives)

*year by the leading hockey club in Canada. There does not
appear to be any outward or visible sign of the championship
at present, and considering the interest that hockey matches now
elicit, and the importance of having the games fairly played under
generally recognized rules, I am willing to give a cup that shall
be annually held by the winning club. I am not quite certain
that the present regulations governing the arrangement of
matches gives entire satisfaction," wrote Lord Stanley. " It would
be worth considering whether they could not be arranged so
that each team would play once at home and once at the place
where their opponents hail from. "*

Lord Stanley attached four more provisos. The challengers had
to post a bond and if victorious, turn the Cup over to any team
that defeated them. Each winning team should, at their own
charge, engrave a silver ring fitted on the Cup, bearing the name

of the team and the year won. The Cup would remain a challenge cup and should not become the property of any team. In case of any question, two trustees, P.D. Ross and John Sweetland, would determine the fate of the Cup. The fifty-seven-year-old Sweetland was the Sheriff of Ottawa. Ross was a newspaper publisher. Should either trustee drop out, the remaining trustee would nominate a substitute.

Not all the conditions would survive. The position of Stanley Cup trustee is now just an honorary position. The Cup is no longer a challenge trophy; it has long since passed into the hands of the NHL, although its care, display, and transportation are coordinated between the league and the Hockey Hall of Fame.

Lord Stanley's decree that the winning team would engrave their name on a silver ring at the base to commemorate every Cup winner probably, more than any other condition, highlights the routine nature of the trophy's commission. Anyone with even a hint of the grandeur the Cup would soon achieve would have guessed that after a decade or so, the Cup would become top-heavy and topple. Commissioning the Cup was, in every way, just a gesture of the day, not a grand movement with an eye to history.

Nonetheless, the Dominion Challenge Cup, almost immediately known as the Lord Stanley Cup and then, the Stanley Cup, was made available for presentation.

None of the preceding facts have ever prompted dispute. Everything that follows has.

According to scores of accounts, the first Cup controversy began in the initial winter of the Cup, 1892-93, and resulted in the Cup going unawarded in its maiden year.

Lord Stanley is said to have hoped that as the top team in the country, the Ottawa team would be named the first winner without having to play for the honor. Hockey historians have long held that the Cup's trustees had other ideas.

"The Stanley Cup is a challenge trophy," the trustees are said to have declared, "and as such it must be won on the ice. If Ottawa wants the Cup, let them win it in competition." The trustees are then said to have ordered the Ottawa team to play

(Hockey Hall of Fame Archives)

Toronto's Osgood Hall club. The Ottawa club refused, the trustees remained adamant, and the Cup was not awarded in the first year it was available.

The Trustees had a Challenge Cup but no team to defend it. The Montreal Amateur Athletic Association team, who were considered champions of the Amateur Hockey Association of Canada, said they would be glad to be remembered as the first Cup winners. The Montrealers successfully defended the Cup in 1894 and everyone went home happy.

There is only one problem with the story. It probably isn't true.

"Pure folklore," said hockey historian James Duplacey, a Toronto-based expert with dozens of hockey books to his credit. "That whole story was created to cover up why Montreal didn't get the trophy until 1894. It's pure fiction."

The story Duplacey claims is bogus originated in The Stanley Cup Story, a seminal bit of Stanley Cup scholarship authored by sports historian Henry Roxborough. There was a dispute between the Ottawa club and Osgood Hall on the terms of a challenge, but Duplacey believes that happened in 1894, not 1893. Duplacey points to the fact there was no mention of a dispute between Ottawa and Toronto teams in any newspaper of the day. P.D. Ross, one of the Cup's first two trustees, owned the *Ottawa Journal* at the time and he made no mention of it. Nor did Charles Coleman, author of the authoritative *Trail of the Stanley Cup*. Scott Young, long one of Canada's most preeminent hockey writers, claimed the dispute happened in 1894, not 1893. For more proof, Duplacey points to the fact that the first comprehensive set of Cup guidelines weren't printed in any newspaper until May 1, 1893, long after the inaugural season was over.

Lord Stanley himself was not on hand to sort the mess out. Late in 1893, the Earl of Derby, Lord Stanley's brother, died in England. That forced Lord Stanley to cut short his tenure in Canada, return to England, and assume his duties as the new Earl of Derby.

Duplacey believes the Cup was actually awarded to the Montreal club in 1893, not, as the history books claim, in 1894. "The decision was made the Montreal AAA would be named champions since they had beaten all comers the previous season. They were 7-1 but they had beaten Ottawa and since Ottawa was the only other team with as good a record as theirs, they were awarded the Cup."

What happened next was the first—and by no means the last—case of Cup lust.

"The trophy was formally presented to the Montreal AAA executive on May 15, 1893, but the hockey club felt they should get the trophy," Duplacey said. " The AAA was a group of rowers and bowlers, but it was a whole year before the club got the trophy because there were battles between the hockey club and the AAA association. The team didn't receive the trophy until February 23, 1894. They were fighting right from the get-go."

What is known as the first Stanley Cup game was played in Montreal's Victoria Rink on March 22, 1894. Montreal beat Ottawa at home 3-1 and were carried off the rink by their supporters. The game was a sellout, with 5,000 people jamming the rink.

Controversies over who should be eligible for challenges dominated the early decades of Cup competition, as did hideous treatment of referees. In 1899, 8,000 people, the biggest hockey crowd ever, crowded into an arena to watch the Winnipeg Victorias play their namesakes, the Montreal Victorias. Montreal had a 3-2 lead late in the second period when Winnipeg players and fans nearly rioted over the decision of referee J.A. Findlay to only assess a slashing minor against a Montreal player. Tired of constant carping from fans and Montreal players, Findlay took off his skates and went home.

Organizers hopped into a horse-drawn sleigh and convinced him to return. He gave the Winnipeg players 15 minutes to return, and when they didn't, he awarded the game to Montreal. It marked the first and only time a Stanley Cup game was awarded on a forfeit.

The Stanley Cup, born on a whim, quickly matured into a trophy worthy of cost and controversy. In early 1905, the Cup was the prize in one of the sport's most elaborate and ill-fated challenges, the standard by which misplaced Cup ambitions would be judged.

A group of players from the northern Klondike, emboldened perhaps by the frontier gold fever that ripped through the region, challenged the finest team in the land, the Ottawa Silver Seven, for the Stanley Cup. The Seven were named for the seven silver nuggets directors paid the team for winning the Stanley Cup. Later renamed the Senators, they won 10 Stanley Cup challenges and in 1950 Canadian sports editors selected them Canada's greatest team in the first half of the twentieth century.

The Dawson City Nuggets, by comparison, were a collection of civil servants and included one teenager and a cast of irregulars. Hockey players, mostly transplanted Easterners, were common in the North during the gold rush and they congregated in Dawson City. Heaven knows, ice was easy to find and the players eventually came to believe that despite their lack of experience and talent, they could somehow challenge the game's best.

Joe Boyle, nicknamed Colonel for his recklessness and daring in navigating boatloads of prospectors through the Whitehorse River Rapids, was the biggest man in Dawson City. The city boasted a fine arena but no real competition, especially for a local team that included one-time Ottawa star Weldy Young. On a trip east, Boyle met with Stanley Cup trustees and submitted a challenge. "Think of it, gentleman," he told the trustees, "a team traveling 4,000 miles in the dead of winter to play a Stanley Cup series. It's a hockey promoter's dream."

Boyle was dead right about that. The town promised each man $1,000 should they return with the Stanley Cup. Amazingly, they won approval from the Cup's trustees to fulfill their challenge.

A 4,400-mile journey started on December 4, 1904, with some men walking, some on dogsled and others, mindful of a rare thaw, riding bicycles. Each man carried his own skates. After a few miles, the wheels on the bikes broke down and everyone walked toward Whitehorse. Each day, the men covered from 33 to 46 miles. Each night, they slept in a Northwest Mounted

Police post. After nine days of walking, they reached Whitehorse, just ahead of a minus -54° cold snap that scuttled any hope of continuing on for five days. Finally, they reached Skagway by railroad. There they found a tiny piece of ice, 40 by 50 feet, on which to practice. Half the surface was covered by sand.

By now, the feet of several of the players were swollen by frostbite. They sailed to Seattle. Then it was Vancouver, where they were greeted by a huge crowd and sent off by train to Ottawa with the cheers still ringing in their ears.

At every stop, well-wishers flooded onto the train, but in Winnipeg the team learned that because of the Silver Seven's league commitments, there would be no rest for the miners when they reached Ottawa. Bad blood began seeping into the series. "We'll default the first game and take care of the champs in the other two," said one miner.

The trip took 25 days in total and when they arrived in Ottawa, any anger was abated by a full-fledged welcome that included dinner and ample drinks at a posh Ottawa club. The Silver Seven sent the visitors home that evening in cutters pulled by ponies.

Surging crowds broke store windows and police had to be called to cut through the crowds and get the day's Governor General and parliamentary power brokers into the arena. But even the miniscule chance of an upset evaporated in light of the brutal scheduling. Devastated by the trip, and, no doubt, by the night before, the Klondikes were steamrolled 9-2 in the first game.

"The visitors were clearly outclassed and while it is true they hardly had the time to get in shape, the form they did show was the most mediocre kind," sniffed an Ottawa newspaper. Upbraided, the Klondikers committed their biggest mistake. The visitors, who averaged what was then a formidable 164 pounds at forward, began speaking of intimidating the Silver Seven. They noted they had limited the great Frank McGee to just one goal in their opening loss.

Three nights later, an angry McGee pumped home 14 goals, including four in a 100 second span, and the locals demolished the visitors 23-2. It was the worst beating in Cup history.

After the game, the Cup suffered perhaps its most famous

indignity. In a riotous celebration, someone got the idea to drop-kick the Cup onto the frozen Rideau Canal. Hockey history records the punter as Harvey Pulford. "I've authenticated that story myself," said longtime Hall of Fame curator Lefty Reid. "He was an outstanding athlete who liked, as many did, to bend his elbow. What isn't true is the idea that it fell into water. It was ice." The next morning, someone remembered the night before and fetched the Cup from the canal.

The Klondikers, meanwhile, continued on a 23-game barn-storming tour of the Maritimes, Quebec, and Ontario, all in the name of earning money for their return trip home. Goalie Albert Forrest, at seventeen, the youngest competitor in Cup history, walked the last 350 miles from Pelly Crossing to Dawson City alone.

The Klondikes' trip was a failure on the ice, but Boyle's promise of widespread publicity had proved true. The famous junket pushed hockey onto the front pages and team operators, anxious to earn this new Cup people were talking about, began supplementing their clubs with hired guns from outside their area. The argument, amateurs versus professionals, is really as old as the Cup itself and it resonated at the Nagano Olympics when NHL players usurped amateurs in search of the men's hockey gold medals.

There is no question Lord Stanley stipulated the Cup should be the prize of amateur players. Still, the distinction is hardly worthwhile since there were no real professional clubs until Lord Stanley, inadvertently, gave hockey's first generation of play-for-pay talents a trophy for which to shoot. While some would say Lord Stanley would have disapproved of professionals and ringers, there was an equally cogent argument on the other side. His trustees had ample opportunity to bar professionals and chose instead to keep the Cup the goal of hockey's finest players.

In March of 1907, an official with the Kenora (Ontario) Thistles became so angry over negotiations between the Cup's trustees and officials from the Montreal Wanderers over the eligibility of a couple of Kenora players, that he threatened to throw the trophy, for the first and only time in the Thistles' possession, into a nearby lake.

Local businessmen sought to bring the Cup's emerging prestige to their towns. A dentist named J.L. Gibson compiled one of the best teams of the time in Houghton, Michigan in 1905-1906 that included the great Cyclone Taylor at rover and Joe Hall at left wing, but the Cups' trustees were unwilling to sanction the game. The games involving mining towns were wild affairs with big money, sometimes as high as $50,000, wagered on teams staffed by imports.

The Renfrew Millionaires were financed not by gate receipts but by the wealth of mine owner Ambrose J. O'Brien and Industrialist J.G. Barnett. Lester and Frank Patrick, Cyclone Taylor, and Newsy Lalonde played for the Millionaires, as did goalie Bert Lindsay, father of Detroit Red Wings' Hall of Famer Ted Lindsay. Taylor is said to have received an astronomical $4,500 to play with the Millionaires, named for the largess of their owners. The Patrick boys got $3,000 each.

In 1910, O'Brien helped form the National Hockey Association, a league composed of the Ottawa Senators, the Montreal Canadiens, Montreal Wanderers, and Toronto Arenas. By now, star players Lester and Frank had gone West and founded the Pacific Coast Hockey Association with teams in British Columbia located in Vancouver, Victoria, and New Westminster. With the best players headed to the professional leagues, NHA teams played Western teams for the Stanley Cup.

Tired of squabbling between franchises, NHA owners met in Montreal in November of 1917 and emerged from the meetings with a new league, the NHL. The first NHL Stanley Cup season, 1917-1918, involved just three teams. Toronto defeated Montreal 10-7 in a two-game total goals series to become the first NHL champions. They retained the Cup by winning three of five games from Vancouver, the Pacific Coast challengers.

The National Hockey League continued to flourish. In 1924, Boston became the first American city to join the NHL. Because

THEY'RE OFF!
WATCH THEIR SMOKE!

1933-34

Buzz Boll, George Hainsworth, Hec Kilrea, Chas Sands, Benny Grant, Bill Thoms, Ken Doraty, Red Horner, Joe Primeau, Alex Levinsky, Harvey Jackson, King Clancy, Andy Blair, Chas. Conacher, Harold Cotton, Ace Bailey, Happy Day, Rube Bannister, Dr. J.W. Rush, Tom Daly, Dick Irvin, Connie Smythe, Frank J Selke.

(Imperial Oil - Turofsky / Hockey Hall of Fame Archives)

so many French Canadians worked in the textile industries, it had always been an excellent hockey town. By 1925, the Pittsburgh Yellow Jackets and New York Americans were in the fold and Chicago, Detroit, and another New York team, the Rangers, were seeking admittance.

The NHL and Pacific Coast Hockey Association became rivals, and it was natural then that the two would stage an annual tournament for the Stanley Cup. The Pacific Coast Hockey Association teams claimed only one Cup, when Victoria upended the Montreal Canadiens to win the Cup in 1925. The rivalry died in 1926 when the Pacific Coast League, by then renamed the Western Hockey League, finally gave in to financial pressures and disbanded, the players heading east.

It had been a rollicking first quarter-century of play for Lord Stanley's little gift but by now, the modern day NHL was taking shape. With it would come a new orbit for the Stanley Cup.

Chapter 5

BAD JOE HALL

The Stanley Cup playoffs have been rescheduled for tragedy and outrageous circumstances. The Colorado Avalanche rescheduled their opening games of the 1999 playoff season and adopted special patches on their uniform as an acknowledgement of the shooting deaths at Columbine school, near Denver. The assassination of Dr. Martin Luther King prompted the postponement of three games during the quarterfinal round of the 1968 playoffs. The New York Rangers-Chicago Blackhawks series was delayed for five days and series between St. Louis and Chicago as well as Minnesota and Los Angeles were also delayed.

Infinitely less tragic circumstances have prompted cancellations and site changes. A squirrel blacked out the Edmonton Oilers bid for a four-game sweep of the Stanley Cup finals in 1988. Edmonton won the first three games against Boston but a squirrel found its way into a hydro box at the old Boston Garden, plunging the arena into darkness. With the score 3-3, the game was declared postponed and Game 4 was reconvened in Edmonton two days later. Buoyed by the home crowd, the Oilers swept the Bruins with a 6-3 win.

Only once has the show not gone on. The Montreal Canadiens won the NHL title in 1919. The custom of the day dictated that the Canadiens would play the Western champs, the Seattle Metropolitans, for the Stanley Cup. The Black Flu, Spanish Influenza, was devastating the continent. To pay for their trip West, the Canadiens barnstormed through the Prairies. In Brandon,

Manitoba, Canadiens' defenseman Joe Hall was given a few days off to visit his family. It was on this hometown visit that Hall is believed to have contracted influenza.

Hall was a fearsome defenseman. When he played for Brandon in the Manitoba Hockey League, a Winnipeg player butt-ended and severely injured the club's goalie. Hall took it upon himself to beat up not only the miscreant but also every member of the Winnipeg team. He was known everywhere as Bad Joe Hall.

The two teams split the first five games with two wins, two losses, and a tie, but Hall and his roommates Bill Couture and Jack McDonald fell ill immediately prior to what could have been the deciding Game 6. The players' fevers ran as high as 105 and Hall died on April 5 at the age of thirty-seven.

The series was declared halted and the deciding game was never played. It marked the first and only time an NHL play-off ended with no decision. No names adorned the Stanley Cup for the 1919 season but one name remains paramount: the fallen Canadien, Bad Joe Hall.

Chapter 6

MISTAKES, THEY MADE A FEW

When he donated the Stanley Cup for challenge play, Lord Stanley set in motion the most unique characteristic of the Cup that would bear his name.

"Each winning team to have at their own charge" he wrote, "engraved on a silver ring fitted on the Cup for the purpose, the name of the team and the year won."

It has never been clarified whether he meant a new ring for every team or whether every ring should also include the name of every player. Still, the Montreal Athletic Association bought a ring and left room for those to follow. By 1902, the ring was completely filled.

Rather than buy a new ring, not an unsubstantial undertaking in 1903, the champion Montreal AAA team carved their name right into the bowl. In a nice gesture of overkill, the Ottawa Silver Seven, themselves no more willing to buy another ring than had been the AAA, engraved not only the team name but also the name of all 10 teams who unsuccessfully challenged their hockey supremacy.

When the Montreal Wanderers won the Cup in 1906, they continued the search for unoccupied space on the Cup and undertook the difficult job of inscribing names on the decorative fluting atop the Stanley Cup bowl. Half the openings were covered by their first win, and they consumed the other half when they defeated a challenge from New Glasgow, Nova Scotia.

As the championships increased, so too did the ingenuity of

the winners. The Kenora Thistles, 1907 champions, found room on the inside of the bowl. When the Wanderers rebounded to reclaim the Cup from Kenora, they used the bottom of the bowl to inscribe the names of their players.

The Wanderers returned as Cup champions in 1908 but, unable to find any more usable space on the original bowl and no doubt tired of inscribing their names on this silly trophy, they declined the honor.

The following year, the Ottawa Senators found victory and the money to commemorate it. They installed a new base, directly under the Cup's silver ring and added a second ring, where the club noted its victory. Reenter the Wanderers. The team that had been either too cheap or too disinterested to spring for a new ring now didn't bother to even carve their names into vast empty areas of the amended trophy. There is no mention on the bowl of the 1910 Wanderers and, for that matter, the 1911 Senators.

The Cup tradition of inscribing names was restored in 1912. Still, that was by no means the end of the logistical headaches. From a paucity of teams on the Cup, trustees were now faced with an overabundance. Between 1915 and 1918, the Ottawa Senators, Portland Rosebuds, and Vancouver Millionaires put their names on the Cup, even though they had not won it. By then, the Cup was no longer a challenge trophy but a series between the two dominant leagues, the NHL/NHA and the Pacific Coast Hockey Association. Ottawa, Portland, and Vancouver had all defeated the defending Cup champions in their league playoffs but lost the Cup in the NHL-PCHA playoff. That didn't stop them from inscribing their names onto the Cup.

The Vancouver Millionaires, who improperly engraved their names in 1918, finally completed the space on the Cup's second ring. According to Toronto-based Cup historian Eric Zweig, no one bothered to inscribe their name on the trophy for the next six years. One season can be explained, as the 1919 series was called off in the wake of the influenza epidemic that killed hundreds of thousands worldwide. But Ottawa's victories in 1920, 1921, and 1923 as well as the Toronto St. Pats' win in

The Cup circa 1925. (Hockey Hall of Fame Archives)

1922 were not recorded on the Cup. No one knows why.

Fittingly, it was the Montreal Canadiens, the all-time leading franchise in Cup wins, who restored a dying tradition and returned the luster to the fading Cup. When the Canadiens swept Ottawa, Vancouver, and Calgary, in 1924, they celebrated their convincing victory with a band encircling the base of the trophy. In a gesture of largess that would become typical of the club's first-class image, each player on the team had his name engraved and it has been thus forever more.

As for mistakes, engravers have made a few. Bob Gainey's name was misspelled in 1975 as Gainy. An "r" was omitted in the name of Montreal Maroons coach and general manager Eddie Gerard's last name on the panel commemorating the club's 1925-26 title. Pete Palangio shows up twice with the 1937-38 Blackhawks, once correctly and another time as Palagio. The name of goaltending great Turk Broda appears twice with the 1941-42 Maple Leafs. Montreal Canadiens' superstar goalie Jacques Plante, the father of the goaltender's face mask, won the Cup five consecutive times from 1956 to 1960. His name is spelled differently each and every time. The 1962-63 Cup champion Leafs are spelled Toronto Maple Leas on the Cup.

When the names of the 1983-84 Oilers were inscribed, swash-buckling owner Peter Pocklington included the name of his father, Basil Pocklington, even though he was unaffiliated with the team. The NHL learned of the move and ordered the name removed. Sixteen Xs obliterated the name.

The Boston Bruins put the name of hard rock defenseman Ted Green on the Cup in 1970, even though Green had suffered a ghastly head injury in a stick-swinging incident in the exhibition season and did not play all year. The league explained away the gesture as a mistake.

Green's inclusion was, in fact, something of a Boston tradition. The Bruins listed goalie Hal Winkler as a member of the 1929 Cup-winning Bruins, even though he did not play a minute that season. Winkler, who led the league in minutes played and shutouts the previous year season, retired in 1928 and the Bruins honored him by designating him as their "sub-goal-tender." The Bruins were punched in as the Bqstqn Bruins in 1971-72. The O was confused for a Q and the mistake could not be corrected.

The last known mistake occurred in 1996, when the name of Colorado Avalanche winner Adam Deadmarsh, inadvertently punched in as Adam Deadmarch, was subsequently corrected.

Chapter 7

LINDSAY'S GREATEST PASS

Over 17 NHL seasons, Ted Lindsay ruled as one of most combative, fiercely competitive players in the often-brutal six-team NHL of the 1940s, 1950s, and early 1960s.

He was Terrible Ted, the cocksure embodiment of a raucous and stellar Detroit Red Wings club that during his tenure included the great Gordie Howe, devastating defenseman Black Jack Stewart, and goaltending legends Terry Sawchuk and Glenn Hall.

Lindsay's courage was incalculable. During a 1956 semifinal series against Toronto, Detroit officials received a threat that Lindsay would be shot, should he appear in Toronto for the third game of the series. That night he engaged in a bloody fight, scored the tying and winning goals and, for his finale, machine-gunned the Toronto crowd with his stick. His face contained the marks and scars of his conviction. Players, fans, and media called him "Scarface."

"Different players will do different things to win," Hall once said. "Ted Lindsay would do anything to win." But beyond the brash exterior, Lindsay was a man of deep principle.

One of those principles was the notion that the Stanley Cup belonged to the fans as well as the players. There was, in those days before Plexiglas, a much closer relationship between players and spectators. Chicken wire kept the pucks from the paying customers at both ends of the ice but no one had thought to wall in the sideboards. The customers leaned against them and even leaned back when the players bumped into the boards. Like the right field denizens at Boston's Fenway Park or Wrigley Field's Bleacher Bums, the spectators kept up a running dialogue with the players.

When the Wings won the Stanley Cup at home in 1955, Lindsay shook hands with NHL president Clarence Campbell and then, rather than just admire the Stanley Cup that sat on the card table, he picked it up and began skating with it. "Mr. Adams and Mr. Campbell were both probably wondering, 'What is that crazy Lindsay doing with the Cup?'" Lindsay recalled from Detroit, "Maybe he's going to throw it away.' But we had great fans and my intent was to get the Cup as close to them as possible. I wanted them to get a closer look, so I took it to the boards and very gradually I worked my way around the rink. The fans paid my salary. I was always very conscious of that."

A few years after that, the Canadiens' Jean Beliveau followed suit by skating the Cup around, and a few springs after that, Leafs' captain George Armstrong is believed to have been the first player to pass the Cup among teammates.

Lanny McDonald, a winner with the Calgary Flames in 1989, says sharing the Cup with spectators, albeit through Plexiglas, is part of the magic, even if his only Cup victory came on the road in Montreal. "It's a player's way of saying, 'Here, it's ours,'" McDonald said, "But it's yours too.'"

"You're saying you (the team) did it and it's yours," said Hall of Famer Mike Bossy, a four-time winner with the Islanders. "But the crowd lives through the season with you, and you're showing them, letting them know, that you went through the season together. It's a way of saying thank you."

Once freed of the card table, the Stanley Cup became a true trophy, one that could be passed not only in front of fans but also among players. Lindsay, on impulse, had broached the idea that rather than standing stolidly on a table, the Cup could be shared. It was the genesis of what is now a Cup tradition, the passing of the Cup from captain to teammates and it carries its own rigorous protocol.

The captain is always the first to receive the Cup from the

commissioner. Then, depending on the decision of the captain, the most deserving player grasps it next.

Bobby Clarke, the heartbeat of the Flyers' championships in 1974 and 1975, remembers grasping the Cup both times. "It's lighter than you think," said Clarke "Of course, at that moment, anything would be light."

Wayne Gretzky won four championships with the Edmonton Oilers and monopolized the record book, but to many, his finest hour came one night in May of 1987 after the Oilers had disposed of the Philadelphia Flyers to win the Cup.

In the previous year's playoff, young defenseman Steve Smith gifted the Calgary Flames with the series-clinching goal when he accidentally banked a shot off goalie Grant Fuhr into his own net. The marker, made even more onerous because it gave the series to the hated Flames, was a devastating blow to Smith. The Oilers rebounded to win the Cup the next year, and in the mad-house of the Northlands Coliseum, Gretzky accepted the Cup from commissioner John Ziegler, pivoted, and then dashed through a scrum of reporters and media, past Fuhr, a vital cog in the Oilers Cup wins, to Steve Smith, on the outside of the scrum. "That night was very special to me," Smith recalled. "It was very emotional. For it to be my first Stanley Cup and then to get the opportunity to hold it before an awful lot of guys who deserved it an awful lot more, it was an unforgettable moment."

When he retired at the conclusion of the 1998-99 season, Gretzky was asked to remember the most significant moment of his career.

"It's no comparison. My first Stanley Cup," Gretzky said. " Every guy who lifted the Cup the first time will tell you the same thing. We all love our first goal. We all love it when the coach says you're going to play in your first game of the NHL. But there's no feeling like lifting that Stanley Cup. It's the greatest thrill in the world. I guess it's like your firstborn child. You always remember it like it was yesterday."

It is that element of inclusion that makes the Stanley Cup unique. Pittsburgh Penguins star Jaromir Jagr, who scored the winning goal in Gretzky's last game and in doing so, declared his ascendancy as the game's premier talent, said winning the Cup would have no meaning were it not for the names of teammates that have twice surrounded his own. "That's the motivation for me, to celebrate a goal, celebrate winning a game, celebrate winning the series, celebrating winning the Cup. Nobody can take that away from you. You're going to have that forever, the fun with your teammates."

In recent years, the captain has handed the Cup to the Conn Smythe winner as the most valuable player in the playoffs. Said Maple Leafs' goalie Glenn Healy, who held the trophy as a New York Ranger in 1994, "It became a signal to go from the Captain to the Conn Smythe winner. Then it usually goes in seniority based on the number of years you put in. If you're a young guy, you certainly aren't third in line."

Who was to receive the Cup from the captain would become an important political consideration. When the Philadelphia Flyers won their Stanley Cups in the early 1970s, Bobby Clarke passed the Cup first to MVP goalie Bernie Parent. One year, Hall of Fame defenseman Denis Potvin passed the Cup to Clark Gillies, his predecessor as Islander Captain, as a gesture of respect for his leadership.

When the Dallas Stars earned the franchise's first-ever Stanley Cup in 1999, Captain Derian Hatcher accepted the Cup from commissioner Gary Bettman. He gave it to Mike Modano, the dominant Star in the series, who passed it to Brett Hull, the owner of the Cup-winning goal. The rest of the procession was mishmash. Joe Nieuwendyk, who won the Conn Smythe Trophy as the most valuable player of the postseason, was the ninth player to hold it.

"On our team, it went from our captain, Scott Stevens, to the two As (assistant captains)," said Ken Daneyko, who celebrated with the New Jersey Devils in 1995. "In our case it was John MacLean, Bruce Driver, and then myself. We did it based on seniority."

Every player seemingly has his own way of describing the feeling of holding the Stanley Cup. "The hour or so after you win the Cup, you're not conscious of your body, you're not conscious of anything else except emotion," said Glenn (Chico) Resch, a winner with the Islanders in 1980. "It was an incredibly different high than playing and just winning a game. When you win a game, it's something that lasts for an hour or two. But after you win the Cup, you want to sustain that feeling because you know, once you go to sleep, that's gone, you're going to get farther and farther away from it. It's like you're chasing this natural high, so you do everything that night to keep that going. It was interesting how it was just a gradual, gradual comedown," said Resch. "It is the ultimate because you can't stay up that long about anything else as you do in this game. For me, it was like more of an atomic bomb. This one, it just kept rolling, and you try to keep it going as long as you could."

"I live in East Norwich (Long Island). The next day was Memorial Day and there was a parade two blocks from my house. I promised my daughter I'd take her to the parade. The parade came up the hill from Oyster Bay Long Island and the Grand Marshal leading the parade was (Islander) Butchie Goring. He's got the same suit on he had on when we won. He had platform heels on, about six or eight inches, but there was Butchie. He had some friends in Oyster Bay, and obviously they didn't go to bed that night. He might be the only guy in history who went from winning the Cup one night to being the grand marshal of a parade the next. Oh, I laughed."

Bobby Clarke, now the Flyers' General Manager, remembers that feeling of not wanting to leave the room in which the cup resides. "When you leave the ice and then leave the room, you know you're moving away from it. And then, in about three days, you're thinking about the next season."

Toronto Maple Leafs' president Ken Dryden won six Cups in his eight years as a member of the Montreal Canadiens. Each one, he said, is both different and similar to the last.

"It really depends on what you went through to win it," Dryden said, "but the basic elements of the experience remained unchanged. As a moment of triumph it's great," said Dryden. "It's that moment of ultimate freedom, where you have license to feel great, you have license to do almost anything and people will not only understand but they will love to watch you do it. You want to celebrate and people want to celebrate with you and you don't want it to stop."

Like Resch, Dryden remembers doing almost anything to keep the moment going. "The moment that it begins to slow down a little bit, you're afraid it's going to stop so you'll speed it up again. The celebration tradition-we won every year but one on the road-was flying back to Montreal. The people at the airport. Heading down to the South Shore to Claude St. Jean's restaurant, spending the rest of the night there. The following day was the parade. And then to a bar called Friday's and then from Friday's to the team party at night and then the following morning to Toe Blake's Tavern at 11 a.m. and then Henri Richard's at 2 p.m. You were always looking for the next place. When Jacques Lemaire opened his place it was "Well, we've got to go to Jacques.' There was always this urge to go to the next place and there was this feeling that the moment you stopped, it would all be over. And then you'd have to go home and the license to feel as you did and to do as you did would be gone, and you'd have to take out the garbage and get back to being everybody else."

For all the emotion, Dryden found commonalities with those outside the sport. Winning, even when winning means the Stanley Cup, is the same everywhere. "When a kid comes up to you or a parent says they've never won a Stanley Cup, I ask 'Have you ever won anything?' They say 'Yeah, we won the peewee football championship.' I tell them, 'That's what it felt like: that incredible excitement, that relief at the end, that desire to be around with their buddy's arm around each others' shoulders, saying great things about each other. If you've had that, that's what it's like," It is a feeling, Clarke said, that accrues with time. "I think you get more benefit and pleasure from winning after you've retired. You've got the time to think about what it took to win it. When you're playing, you celebrate for three or four days and then it's time to get ready for the next year. At least now the players get it in July and August so at least they can relive it again. We saw it for one night at a party at Mr. Snider's (owner Ed Snider's) house, and that was it."

"Growing up, you dream of playing in the NHL and you dream you're going to be part of a championship," said Bobby Orr, considered by many the greatest NHL player ever. "You watch the Leafs and the Canadiens on television with the Stanley Cup. And then one day, you're following Johnny Bucyk around the ice with the Stanley Cup. It is," he said, in the words that all those who describe it invariably return to, "a dream come true."

(Imperial Oil / Hockey Hall of Fame Archives)

Chapter 8

THE SNUB

It has been 50 years and mostly what Doug McKay remembers of his Stanley Cup moment is his dad. "That," he said, "and knocking a big New York defenseman on his ass."

McKay's name is not on the Stanley Cup but he has never sought to have the Cup changed. Old hockey players, like old soldiers, break down into two groups: those who like to speak of the past and those who do not. McKay does not, or at least does not offer to, but his is one of the Cup's untold stories.

McKay believes his name is not included because of a grudge, one between McKay and longtime Detroit Red Wings' coach and general manager Jack Adams.

McKay, who lives in his hometown of Hamilton, Ontario, has not checked the Cup for his name, even though it sits an hour's drive away at the Hockey Hall of Fame in Toronto. "I'd never bother to go look for my name," he said. "It was a different era. In those days, after you played, you went home. Playing for it was a neat honor but that was it."

Doug McKay was a minor league left-winger in the days of the six-team league, a time where the better minor league teams could have competed handsomely against the lower tier of NHL clubs. He was the property, as fitting a noun as any, of the Detroit Red Wings, who were managed by the despotic Jack Adams. The Wings were gunning for the Stanley Cup in 1950 but a spate of injury problems had temporarily decimated the club.

The Wings had a championship minor league team in Omaha

and Adams sent for three reinforcements. McKay was one of them and he played one game of the Stanley Cup finals against New York in Toronto. The Rangers had been booted out of old Madison Square Garden by the circus and as unbelievable as it seems today, they decided to play their second and third home games at Maple Leaf Gardens. For McKay, the venue change meant his dad could see him play. That, and the hit are all Doug McKay remembers of his one NHL game. By the next game, the Wings roster had stabilized and at the behest of the team's veterans, limping regulars were inserted back into the lineup over the new kids from Omaha. Adams was loath to use McKay anyway; the two feuded nearly from the day McKay was signed by the Wings.

Stanley Cup rules dictate that a player who appears in the Stanley Cup final should have his name on the Cup. The club submits the list and for whatever reason, Doug McKay's name was not on it. He never played another NHL game but ground out a lengthy career as a minor-league player and later, a minor league coach.

McKay is seventy now and he doesn't believe the snub was an honest mistake. "It doesn't surprise me. Jack Adams and I never got along." He laughs at the idea of a correction. He played; he knows it. The Stanley Cup won't change his mind. "Listen," he says without a hint of regret, "there is nothing as far away as the past."

Chapter 9

BASHIN' BILL

It begins on Friday, August 24, 1951. Bill Barilko stood at the door of his mother's bedroom in the early morning light and stared at the floor. "Goodbye Mom," he said. "See you Sunday night."

Fay Barilko would always regret what happened next. She said nothing. She was angry. The night before, she had begged her son Billy not to embark on a flying fishing trip from the family home in Timmins, Ontario, north to the pristine waters of James Bay. "I was so angry" she recalled later. "My husband die on Friday five years before. I say, 'Billy don't go. Not on Friday. I no like Friday.'"

The night before, his sister Anne had tried to talk him out of the trip as well. "It was the distance," she said. "It seemed like such a long way to go to fish, especially since there was so much good fishing around here. And to go by plane..."

"I don't know why everyone is making such a big fuss about this," Barilko said. Then he borrowed $100 from his sister to pay for the trip, grabbed the lunch she packed for him and headed off. It was that way with Bill Barilko, Bashin' Bill. He liked action and ventured deep in enemy territory so often, the Toronto Maple Leafs' coach Joe Primeau had warned he would fine his dashing young defenseman $100 for every time he crossed the opponent's blue line. And Bill Barilko just went ahead and did it anyway.

Barilko was flying with a friend, bound for Fort Rupert, a couple of hours away. It was his last chance for fishing before training camp, and as a freshly minted Stanley Cup hero, the season

Bill Barilko (flying over ice) and the famous overtime, Stanley Cup-winning goal.
(Imperial Oil-Turofsky / Hockey Hall of Fame Archives)

would soon be demanding his full attention.

Five years before, as a nineteen-year-old rookie, Bill Barilko hit the NHL like a hurricane.

He was just a rookie, handsome as any actor, brash and full of confidence. He came to the Maple Leafs through a contact of owner Conn Smythe. Barilko was playing in the minors in Hollywood, California, and a spate of injuries had knocked most of Smythe's usual defenders out of the lineup.

Smythe heard about Barilko and phoned a former NHL player named Tommy Anderson, who was the playing coach in Hollywood. "He's pretty green," Anderson told Smythe, "but he's a big fast boy, not afraid of anyone and he learns fast." Barilko reported to work and told Smythe his search for help was over. "Don't worry about the Kid," he said to newspapermen. "This is something I've always dreamed of and I'm aiming to stay around."

Billy the Kid did just that. The following season, he served 147 minutes in penalties to lead the league, and took his place among

The Maples' Bill Barilko shares the penalty box with Gordie Howe.
(Imperial Oil-Torofsky / Hockey Hall of Fame Archives)

the game's most devastating hitters. They called him Bashin'
Bill. Montreal Canadiens' star Elmer Lach, for one, considered
him the hardest hitter in the league. "When he hits you, he
hurts you." Lach said.

Still, Barilko remained a small town boy. Every summer, when
he hit Timmins, he knocked on the doors of the neighbors he
knew as a boy. In the fall, he would repeat the process to say
goodbye. He lavished gifts on his family: the family's first
refrigerator, and furs for his mother and his sister.

Going into the 1951 playoffs, Barilko was already a three-time
Cup winner. The Leafs and the Montreal Canadiens squared off
in the 1951 final. For the first time, every game was determined
in overtime. The Leafs were leading the series three games to one
but seemed destined to lose game five and return to Montreal

for Game 6 when the Leafs' Tod Sloan scored with just 37 seconds left to play, to send the game into overtime.

Barilko was spectacularly effective against Montreal and was credited in the first game with diving across the net to deflect a sure goal by Rocket Richard. Now he was ready to step into hockey history.

Bill Barilko's Stanley-Cup winning goal began as a series of seemingly innocuous errors, each capitalized upon by wingers Harry Watson and Howie Meeker. The play began with three minutes left in the first overtime with the puck slipping off Watson's stick in the slot. It hit the skate of Butch Bouchard, the Canadiens' kingpin defenseman. Rocket Richard, seeing the dependable Bouchard with the puck, began to break out of the Canadiens' zone. The normal play for Barilko would have been to retreat and shadow the spectacular Richard into the Leafs' zone, for Bouchard would surely put the puck on the Rocket's stick. Instead, Barilko veered toward a spot between the face-off circle and the two Canadiens, and intercepted the clearing pass on his backhand. Barilko nearly collided with the Leafs' astonished center Cal Gardner before whipping the puck over fallen Montreal goalie Gerry McNeil and in that flash of audacity, Bill Barilko had made himself a Stanley Cup hero.

The picture of Barilko hurdling toward the ice and the puck soaring above fallen Montreal goalie Gerry McNeil remains one of the most identifiable in hockey history.

And so early on the morning of August 24, the hockey hero got on the plane, piloted by Dr. Henry Hudson, a Timmins dentist, for Seal River in James Bay.

The fishing, as Bill Barilko had hoped, was spectacular. At Rupert House on James Bay, they gassed up and headed home. Bad weather was forecast and the two wanted to get home to freeze their catch of char. Barilko didn't care; he disliked eating fish and would have gladly given his share away. The pontoons in the yellow Fairchild 24 bush plane were overloaded, and witnesses at Rupert House said the plane took off awkwardly due to the load.

That moment near the water was the last anyone would see of the two men alive. The flight was 236 miles and the wind at 2,000 feet was 55 mph. Headwinds would cut their speed to 25 mph and with only 50 gallons of gas on a plane loaded with fish, they couldn't come close to completing the 236-mile trip with the fuel they had on board. On Monday morning, Anne Barilko got a phone call saying her brother hadn't made it in on Sunday night.

The search for the two men was one of the biggest ever conducted in Canada. It combined the Royal Canadian Air Force, the Ontario Department of Lands and Forests, and private planes. A $10,000 reward was offered by the Maple Leaf Gardens for anyone locating Barilko and Hudson. Anne and her mother drove north to stand by, waiting for the news, but none came. There was initial hope. Barilko was an experienced woodsman. The two had fishing equipment and that might help them garner food, had they landed safely. After five days, the two women went home. With no bodies or wreckage uncovered, the fate of the two went unconfirmed.

The Leafs cancelled their August victory dinner. "There is still hope that somehow, somewhere, Bashin' Bill will come bouncing back," wrote a Toronto columnist, "but the days pass all too swiftly and hope has grown dim. The vast Northern Ontario bush country knows the answer to what happened to Bill Barilko but the silence has become all too ominous."

Periodically, a wild rumor would surface. The most whimsical had Bill Barilko teaching hockey to Russians behind the Iron Curtain. For half a dozen years after the crash, every spring and fall, the major newspapers in Toronto would call the family and speculate. Finally, Anne Barilko called them, begging not to stir her mother's hopes again. "It was devastating," said Anne, "but Mom always had hope. Every year she would take Billy's suits and sports jackets, she would air them, hanging them outside in the fresh air, thinking that he would be home. She was hoping that he had amnesia. She often said, 'they haven't proved to me that he's dead.'"

That silence would not lift for 11 years and the Leafs' string of Stanley Cups vanished as irrevocably as did Bill Barilko.

In the summer of 1962, a man named Garry Fields was flying between Cochrane and Moosonee. "I saw the sun reflecting off something through the trees, " Fields would tell police. "My passenger said it was just a well-known wreck so I didn't mark my map. When I got back and learned the known wreck was 40 miles off my line, we started to think about Barilko. Another helicopter and two aircraft and myself spent three days flying that line. By June 6, the others had moved a bit away from the line. When I found the spot again, I saw that you had to be directly over the place before you could see anything. I threw out toilet paper to mark the place. There were no landmarks and no scrapes on the trees." The plane's wings had snapped off when they hit a large spruce tree. Branches folded back and the fuselage drove through and down through the trees, burying itself in the mushy forest floor. Then the trees snapped forward and folded over the burning wreck, sealing the two men from view and shrouding in mystery the death of Bill Barilko. "They must have stalled and gone straight down," Fields said. "We sent for the police and moved men in. We found the skeletons still strapped in their seats but the only sign of clothing was a zipper off one of the garments. What I had seen was a pontoon stuck in the ground."

The news came as both a blow and a gift to Fay Barilko. She knew the worst, but at least she knew. "My God, " she said. "Why couldn't this have happened long ago?" Bill Barilko was buried beside his father in Timmins. "She never got over it," said Anne Barilko. "She cried every day. After a while, we told her she had to get over it, but she never could."

Chapter 10

AT HOME WITH HENRI

The Stanley Cup has many suitors but one longtime favorite. Had the Montreal Canadiens moved sooner to award a Stanley Cup ring for each title, Henri Richard would have had a ring for each digit and one to spare. Richard's 11 Stanley Cups is a record, and with two consecutive Cups now considered the late-century version of a hockey dynasty, it looms as a mark for the ages.

Both Richard and Boston Celtics' star Bill Russell have won 11 titles. Longtime New York Yankees catcher Yogi Berra leads Major League Baseball Players with 10 world championships, while Bart Starr is one of a handful of NFL stars to take home five crowns.

There is a lovely irony in this; the tallest procession of Stanley Cups belongs to one of the smallest men to play the game. Henri Richard stood five-foot-seven and at his burliest, weighed 160 pounds. He was not the game's best player, not even, in the estimation of most, the best hockey player in the Montreal household where he grew up. That title belonged to his older brother Maurice, the great 'Rocket' Richard, hockey's first 50-goal scorer and to many the most electrifying player to ever pick up a hockey stick.

They called Henri 'the Pocket Rocket,' or just 'Pocket,' and aside from being from the same household, the Richard brothers had little in common. Henri was only six when Maurice, older by 15 years, married and moved out of the family's working class Montreal home. The brothers see each other occasionally at events but do not visit regularly. While fiercely proud of each other, they are, like many siblings separated by a wide age disparity, casual friends who retain family links.

Richard's father worked as a railroad carpenter and he and his wife Alice had six children, Maurice the second eldest and Henri, the youngest. "We had no money," Henri Richard has said. "My mother would buy a ham on Sunday and we would have it through the week. There was no meat on Friday and we would have to wash in a tub. Like most poor kids, we didn't know any different."

The questions for Henri Richard began as soon as he began playing hockey. Could he become another Maurice? Certainly, he was gifted with a wonderful skating stride and an inarguable gift for the game but there was always the question of size. At sixteen, Henri weighed less than 100 pounds and the more hockey he played, the harder he found it to gain weight. Uncomfortable with the comparisons with his brother, he told people he had no ambition to be hockey player. Instead, he said, he would be a bricklayer, just like one of his sister's boyfriends. But inside, he knew better. "I knew I always wanted to be a hockey player," he said.

By the age of nineteen, he had filled out into an athlete but he built on the differences between himself and the other players. If he was smaller than the rest, he was also more nimble and unencumbered by excess weight. It seemed he could skate forever. At his third NHL camp, the Canadiens signed him. "We had no choice," said coach Toe Blake. "He was outplaying all the veterans."

Richard proved his worth immediately and scored 19 goals as a rookie but he was painfully shy and reserved in English. "Does Henri speak English?" a reporter once asked the bilingual Blake. "I don't even know if he speaks French," came Blake's reply.

Once in his rookie season, Henri wandered around downtown Boston, looking for the Garden. His halting English did not allow him to ask for directions. He would say "Me too" in restaurants after teammates ordered, and then eat whatever came. His humility was so great, it took him 10 years to feel at home enough to shave in the Canadiens' dressing room.

Team success would come quickly enough. Richard arrived just in time to have a hand in the Canadiens' record five Stanley Cups from 1956-60. A terrific scorer in junior, he became more noted as a playmaker in the NHL. Twice he led the league in assists.

The Canadiens won again in 1965, and in 1966 Richard scored the Stanley Cup winner in overtime against Detroit.

Richard's game matured splendidly. Because of his skating ability, Richard could spend his nights lined up against the opposition's best players. He killed penalties effortlessly and night in and night out, the Canadiens' smallest player was also its most fierce.

"He was the same player every night," said John Ferguson, the club's feared longtime enforcer. "It didn't matter if we were playing in Chicago or Boston or Detroit."

Richard won his eighth Cup in 1968 and another in 1969. In 1971 he scored the tying and winning goals in a 3-2 Game Seven win over the Chicago Blackhawks in the Stanley Cup finals. Richard, by now the team's captain, would score six play-off goals in 1973 as the Canadiens stormed to another Cup, Richard's 11th and final. At the age of thirty-eight, he enjoyed a 19-goal season but after scoring just three times the following season, he retired.

He had played 19 seasons and by some measures had even bettered his prodigious brother. Henri's 1,046 points was 81 points more than Maurice's total and he finished with three more Cups. The player who grew up being told he was too small played at least 50 games in every season but his last one.

The business world was similarly conquered. Richard ran an immensely successful bar and restaurant for 26 years and now, comfortably retired at sixty-three, he winters in Florida where he has developed a passion for tennis.

As for his 11 Cups, Henri Richard is modest. "I admit it," he has said. "I was lucky. Had I been in any other city, New York or Chicago, I wouldn't have won nearly as many." It is, he reckons, just a case of right place in the right time.

The truth is far more telling. Great men like Henri Richard find the way to the right place. They make their time the right time.

Chapter 11

THE GOLDEN BOOK

In hindsight, the Stanley Cup seems brilliantly managed.

Deliberate decisions were made along the way to make the Cup the most prestigious sporting trophy in North America, even in the world. The inclusive nature of the Cup, the way it accommodates every name, the perfection of its symmetry, the glory of a Cup presentation, and the victory lap by the winners, everything about the Stanley Cup has the aura of careful and studied management. And then, serendipity steps forward, and the truth comes out.

In this case, serendipity takes the form of a file at the Hockey Hall of Fame, accidentally uncovered by archives staff in the summer of 1999. "We just found it," said director Phil Pritchard, "when we were moving some other files."

The material was mostly personal correspondence, much of it involving former Stanley Cup trustees J. Cooper Smeaton and P.D. Ross. It shows the trustees and in one case, the NHL, to be well-intentioned but willing to make two spectacularly poor choices.

The first, and potentially the most damaging, had to do with the Cup itself. Imagine a much smaller Stanley Cup, perhaps half the size. Instead of the names on the Cup's rings, a book with the names of past winners would be located in the base of the Cup.

In a letter to fellow Cup trustee P.D. Ross, dated April 23, 1946, J. Cooper Smeaton suggested the old 'elephant leg' Cup should be replaced by a revamped Cup that featured what would come to be known as the Golden Book. "As you know," wrote

Smeaton, "the Cup now rests on a very ugly-looking elongated base and it occurred to me that it might be possible to get (Montreal jeweler) Henry Birks, for instance, to design a nice big base which would permit space for sufficient shields on which could be engraved the name of the club and the year and have sort of a Golden Book made up with perhaps a copy of the (Lord Stanley's) Deed of Gift in it along with some history of the Cup, in which the names of the players on each team winning the cup could be inscribed rather than their names on the silver bands now placed around the base.

In this way, the Cup would look very much more dignified and would be a Cup instead of a long, ungainly base with the Cup perched on it. This would naturally involve some expense but I think the idea could be sold to the league and that they would foot the bills." The idea found favor with Ross, one of the Cup's two original trustees, who proposed returning the Cup to its original state and enshrining the names of the winning players in the Golden Book.

"Regarding the Cup itself, I make this suggestion," Ross wrote. "In preference to encumbering it with more shields, and in order to get rid of the tower structure, why not have Birks make a new base, with a receptacle in the base for a golden book to record all the past and prospective winnings of the Cup. The book would only need to be of moderate size, a hundred pages or so with the base detachable from the cup of course, for purpose of transportation. If the NHL balked about paying for an appropriate new base and golden book, I would cheerfully pay the bill myself." Luckily, there would be opponents to such a drastic redesign.

"It must stay as it is, it must be preserved even with scratches," Lester Patrick wrote to then NHL president Clarence Campbell in 1947. "My name was on there 40 years ago (with the Montreal Wanderers) and I don't want that interfered with." Disaster would be averted when Carl Petersen was asked to redesign the Cup. Petersen broadened the bands and kept the names of the winning players, thereby preserving the Cup's most distinctive asset.

Lester Patrick, meanwhile, would become an important Cup

patron. The presentation of the Cup to the winning club's captain—the crowning moment of any celebration—was in doubt, according to a series of letters between Smeaton and league executive and past president Mervyn "Red" Dutton. When the Montreal Canadiens won the Cup in Boston in 1958, rowdy fans shouted down the presentation, prompting officials to conclude the Cup should not be handed over to the winning captain after it had been won.

"The disgraceful behavior of the fans at the end of the final game for the Stanley Cup in Boston last Sunday when the president of the league Mr. Clarence Campbell endeavored to present the Cup, confirmed my thinking in connection with the presentation of the Cup and that is that no presentation should ever be made on the ice at the conclusion of any Cup series," Smeaton wrote. "After all, the Cup is the emblem of the World Championship and there should be some dignity in connection with the presentation. I am not too fussy as to who makes the presentation, but I think it should be done either at a public function such as a banquet or a private club dinner."

Dutton agreed wholeheartedly. "I know exactly what you mean, as I watched the game on television and the disregard for the ceremony of presenting the Stanley Cup has happened many times in the past and I believe that it is now time for you and I to suggest to the National Hockey League some way to eliminate the shumozzle in the presentation to the Champions of the Stanley Cup...invariably there was always a banquet at the home of the Stanley Cup winners and I feel that the Governors of the National Hockey League ought to cooperate not only for the publicity but for the dignity that the Stanley Cup must hold."

League president Clarence Campbell, shaken by the Boston experience, also wanted to end the on-ice presentation. "I feel that the trophy should be ready and available for display immediately following the game under conditions that would ensure that it would not be damaged in any way and that it should be presented to the winning team either in their dressing room afterward or at a special victory dinner, if one is organized, or, failing that, at the All Star Dinner at the commencement of the next season. I have no firm conviction about which of these ideas would be best but I am sure any one of them would be better than what we have had recently."

No one knows why the league changed its mind and continued the on-ice presentation. Perhaps improvements in the public address systems or the objections of television officials convinced them otherwise. We do know that every June, hockey fans should be grateful the shumozzle was allowed to continue.

Chapter 12

MUTUAL FRIENDS

This is a story about three men, three coaches, all connected by a friend.

During 10 separate summers they carved Toe Blake's name into the Stanley Cup.

Eight of those occasions came with Blake coaching the Montreal Canadiens. Only Blake's protégé Scotty Bowman has coached a team to as many professional championships.

Blake's father was a nickel miner in the town of Coniston just outside Sudbury in rugged Northern Ontario, and the Blakes were as tough as the ore their father dug from the earth. Toe Blake's real name was Hector. His baby sister, Margaret, who mispronounced his name Hec-tor into Hec-Toe, coined Toe. Toe was the oldest in a family of 11 children crammed into a four-room company home. Four of Toe's siblings died in infancy. Nails in the walls served as closets. Blake moved steadily up the hockey ladder, first in Sudbury, then later playing senior hockey in Hamilton, Ontario and then with the Canadiens' arch-rival, the Montreal Maroons, the team for which he won his first Cup in 1935. The Canadiens acquired him in February of 1936 and Blake would go on to have a long career as the corner man and sidekick to superstar Maurice Richard. Twice Blake scored Stanley Cup winning goals before a badly broken leg ended his career when he was 35.

Blake turned to coaching and, aside from a brief stint as a coach/general manager in the Quebec Senior League, he was on

Toe Blake, center, with Jean Beliveau and Maurice Richard.
(*Sports Revue* / Hockey Hall of Fame Archives)

the Canadiens' payroll from the day they acquired his playing rights to the day he died. Handed the reins to the team in 1955, he immediately led the club to five consecutive Stanley Cups, always by stressing team.

"I remember his first meeting," said Jean Beliveau, the blue-print for the elegant team captain and a 10-time Cup winner. "He looked around the dressing room and said 'I've got some great hockey players here. But unless we play as a team, it won't matter.'"

Blake was a brilliant coach, gruff, demanding and intuitive with a prodigious memory and a shallow hold on his temper.

Blake sometimes smashed articles in the dressing room to get his players' attention but had a policy of never embarrassing them through the press or in public view. When he reproached a player during a game, he did so while looking up at the scoreboard. The public and media never knew. He believed in building a player's esteem as well as breaking it. Blake had a team rule forbidding players from carrying their suitcases. "When you play for the Montreal Canadiens," he said, "you travel first class."

"Toe was the ultimate coach," said longtime Canadiens' enforcer John Ferguson. "He had a memory like an elephant and he treated the players like men. He had a great feeling behind the bench and masterminded the game in a way nobody has ever been able to." Every player, from the lowliest scrub to the most exalted star had a distinct and well-defined role. Every speech, every dressing room exhortation preached the value of team.

"I played for Toe for 13 years," said Beliveau, "and there's no doubt that he had the greatest ability to get the most out of his players that I have ever seen."

Blake was so competitive; his daughter Joan couldn't finalize her wedding in May of 1958 because if the Canadiens didn't beat Boston in the finals, none of the players would be invited. They did, and the wedding went off flawlessly.

Blake coached the Canadiens to his 10th and 11th championships in 1966 and 1968 but by now, agents and the league's expansion from six to 12 teams was eroding the coach's traditional hold on power. The game was changing and Blake, so essential to its development, could not. He retired in 1968 and when his wife Betty died of cancer five years later, the Canadiens moved back into the center of his life. He was an honored alumni; the club kept him on the payroll as an advisor and every day a car was dispatched to pick him up and drive him to the rink.

It was at the Forum that Blake began talking with the youngish coach of the Montreal Junior Canadiens, a headstrong, taciturn young man named Scott Bowman. The two became good friends. "We used to talk for hours," Bowman said. "Our offices weren't very far apart. He had a great mind for the game and if you listened, you could learn a lot."

Bowman would later coach the Canadiens to five Cups using the principles he had learned from Blake. He, too, stressed team and he, too, was sharp-tongued and decisive. The student had learned well.

By the late 1980s, friends began noticing Blake's difficulties in telling stories he had often recounted with ease. Doctors said he had Alzheimer's Disease, and the greatest coach of any era spent the final years of his life dozing in a wheelchair at a private nursing home. To the end, the Canadiens operated as his surrogate family and arranged and helped subsidized his care. Toe Blake died May 17, 1995, but his reach extended past death. While Bowman and Blake had conducted their chalk talks over coffee, a few thousand miles to the west in Edmonton, Alberta, another coach worked with another protégé.

Ray Hitchcock coached his boy Ken in hockey and baseball. He was his son's finest mentor, recognizing that Ken would resist any new endeavor, like hockey or golf, but once challenged, would work tirelessly to succeed. He had a way with his son, the same way Ken—coach of the 1999 champion Dallas Stars—would have with others.

"He knew I wanted to do those things, but I would whine and snivel and not get them done and find a way for them not to be successful," said Hitchcock. "But he found a way to deal with me." Ken Hitchcock's life was full and uncomplicated. He lived in a middle-class part of Edmonton with two younger siblings. But when Ken was fourteen, Ray died of an inoperable cancer in his back. Hitchcock's life swung radically when he lost his dad. His mom Janet took a job as a receptionist and remarried. The family fragmented.

"I had a lot of bitterness," Hitchcock said. "My mother married a person I didn't like at all. I couldn't compare him to my dad. I just kind of left the family. I was seventeen."

Hitchcock got a job selling hockey equipment to local teams for an Edmonton sporting goods store and turned his attention to coaching hockey. He coached minor hockey for 10 years in

Edmonton and his Sherwood Park Midgets posted a 575-65 mark. Hitchcock graduated to the Western League's Kamloops Blazers and pushed them to a stunning .693 winning percentage over six years.

That success caught the eye of Bob Gainey, the coach and GM of the Dallas Stars. Gainey's coach for his five Stanley Cup victories in Montreal had been Scotty Bowman. Gainey saw in Hitchcock 'the Montreal way.'

"What Ken produces is a work ethic," Gainey said. "It's a level of commitment to produce, and produce consistently. It's always looking for another place to drag one person up, which drags the whole team up." Frustrated by an inability to deliver those very elements, Gainey dropped the coaching reins from his portfolio and promoted Hitchcock in January 1996.

Gainey, like Bowman and Blake, implemented a heavy pressure fore-check system, consistently turned over four lines, and stressed the role of situational players such as face-off and penalty-killing maestro Guy Carbonneau and defensive forward Dave Reid.

Under Hitchcock, Mike Modano, formerly a gifted perimeter player, became one of the league's best two-way forwards and the dominant figure in the 1999 Stanley Cup finals.

"It's a hardworking, hardskating system that's in-your-face and that's been our identity the last couple of years," said Modano. "It's a 60 minute game, and anything less is unacceptable to Hitch and a lot of the players." Scotty Bowman and Toe Blake could not articulate winning hockey any better.

While Hitchcock insists his office door is always open, the player doesn't enjoy the same latitude for public criticism. When Brett Hull complained to a Dallas newspaper about limited ice time, Hitchcock pulled him into his office for a brief recitation of one fact: "We don't do this here." Toe Blake couldn't have done it better. Hull, playing with two badly injured groin muscles, provided the winning goal in triple overtime as the Stars beat Buffalo in six games to gain the Stanley Cup.

And so, in the summer of 1999, there was a meeting of generations and of values.

The meeting had been arranged through Bob Gainey, who in turn had been introduced to the same friend by Scotty Bowman whose acquaintance with the friend had been eased by a great man named Toe Blake. The friend's name, of course, was Stanley.

Chapter 13

A HERO NAMED WALLY

She is sixty-four now and she is sure she will not remarry. Once you've lived with a good man, a man like Wally Harkness, you narrow your focus to those men whose qualities can match his and in doing so punch your own ticket to a single life. He was that good a man.

"There have been a few attachments," said June Harkness from her condo in Aurora, just north of Toronto. "I was even engaged once but in the end, you expect too much."

There is a picture of Wally, among her favorites shots, on the den wall beside her television. It shows him at work, in a smart suit and a thin tie, handsome as the day they met at a dance when they were both 23. He is holding the Stanley Cup, of all things, and is surrounded by the Hart and Conn Smythe Trophies. The photo was a gift from the Toronto Star, which is a bit outside the usual protocol in the often-strained relations between police and media. But then, Wally Harkness wasn't just any cop.

"In retrospect," said June, "I was so lucky to know him. So many people liked him. He was an honest cop. The crooks liked him, the lawyers liked him, and the newspapermen liked him."

June had rheumatic fever as a girl and rheumatoid arthritis as a woman so children were out of the question. Instead, they had the horses. In his off hours, she and Wally bred horses on a farm outside Toronto. He built the barn himself and while they loved being at the farm on weekends, they stayed in the city through Wally's work shifts.

June Harkness' hero, Wally, with the trophies "left in his driveway."
(author's collection)

Wally had one rule. "He never talked about work because he was afraid that if I knew what he was doing, that might put me at risk," June said. "So I never asked." Not even one morning in December of 1970 when she went downstairs in the couple's bungalow and found the Stanley Cup as well as a host of other trophies. "I never touched them but I looked at them for a long time," she remembered.

The trophies were in her basement because thieves had learned the painful truth about the Stanley Cup. While rich men will spend millions of dollars to win it, while athletes will lay their bodies in the way of sticks and pucks and skate blades to gain it, the Stanley Cup is essentially valueless to the undeserving.

Ransoming it is ridiculously complex and accelerates both the chances of arrest and the severity of the charges. It can't be displayed because word would ultimately reach the authorities.

The Cup was stolen for the first time in 1907 when the champion Montreal Wanderers left it at the home of a photographer. A young man stole it out of the photographer's studio, hoping to earn a ransom for its return. Nobody wanted it so the thief, shame-faced, returned it.

The Cup was in a plastic case at the Chicago Stadium in 1961 during the Stanley Cup finals when a man broke the small lock, picked up the Cup and teetered toward the door. The man said he was merely trying to "return the Cup to where it belongs... Montreal." Security people stopped him, a better lock was installed, and the man was not charged. He never knew how lucky he was.

In January of 1970, the original Stanley Cup collar was stolen. The collar, a three-tiered base that supported the bowl and was minted in 1925, carried the names of Cup winners from 1923-1927. The collar bounced around between crooks like a hot potato for seven years. Police found it, still in the original glass case and wrapped in brown paper, at the rear of a Toronto dry cleaning business. Police were acting on a tip when they searched the rear of the business. The bands had been circulated "around the criminal underworld," said Sergeant Robert Morrison. "Several people have had it and the cleaning store is where it came to rest. It just looked like a Christmas package when we picked it up."

Someone could not resist one final temptation. Several names, presumably the thieves or their friends, were scratched in alongside those of famous hockey players King Clancy and Jack Adams. The names were rubbed out by a tinsmith just hours after the rings were returned.

A band of Montreal college students were the most recent inductees of the rogue's gallery of Stanley Cup thieves. In March of 1977, seven students from the University of Montreal staged what was certainly the most pitiably inept attempt to lift the

Cup. Custodian Ray Paquet was near the rear of the building when he noticed a group of young people near the Cup. At least three wore hats and gloves, and a blue backpack was leaning against a wall.

Paquet noticed the arm of the locking mechanism was bent and distended, and as he inspected the Cup's case, the seven slinked to the exit. Paquet dashed upstairs, informed curator Lefty Reid, and went outside to check the license plate number of the getaway car. By then, two of the five had left in another vehicle, but Paquet watched the remaining driver open the blue backpack, pull out a hammer and place it in the trunk of the car.

Police arrived quickly and the students made no attempt to flee. Police found a briefcase in the trunk that contained 30 photos of the entrance and escape route for the theft, closeups of the security case and the electric eye security system. "Not your normal tourist-type shots," Reid chuckled later. The students admitted they were taking part in a scavenger hunt and after several hours of questioning, police let the students off with a warning.

Today, the Cup is removed every evening after closing time from its pedestal at the Hockey Hall of Fame and sealed in a vault. The usual array of burglar alarms and motion detectors are in place to protect the Cup from harm.

But in 1970, when Wally Harkness would come into the picture, thieves were aided and abetted by the fact that security at the longtime home of the Cup, the old Hockey Hall of Fame in Toronto, on the site of the Exhibition Grounds, was lax to the point of laughable. "My staff consisted of one caretaker," said Reid. "We had no security at all. All it required was someone to break in."

Sometime between closing Friday and opening Saturday, December 7, 1970, thieves entered the Hall and stole the Stanley Cup, Hart, and Conn Smythe trophies. It was not a sophisticated heist. The thieves—police knew there were at least two because of the weight of the other trophies taken and the difficulty of lifting the 100 pound case—tried breaking in one door but gave up after breaking a glass pane and damaging a lock.

They went to another corner of the building, twisted out a lock cylinder to gain access to the Cup, and disappeared.

What the thieves did not know, what only a handful of people knew, was that they hadn't made off with the original Stanley Cup. Three years before, concerned about the growing fragility of the Cup, league president Clarence Campbell had quietly authorized the creation of a replica bowl. While the thieves were making away with what they believed to be the Cup, the real bowl was sitting on top of the desk of silversmith Carl Petersen in his Montreal office.

The news that the stolen Cup was in fact a replica vaporized what little bargaining position the thieves had left. "We have all the original parts of the Stanley Cup except a couple of bands (stolen earlier)," Campbell told the media. "Nothing of historic value is missing."

Wally Harkness, then a detective-sergeant on the Toronto Police Force, was the perfect man to track the Cup. He had contacts, he was trustworthy and likeable. A good, honest cop. Within a day, he knew the identity of the thieves. But the men who had stolen the Cup were nervous. "I remember the police telling us that the thieves had threatened to drop the Cup into the Lake (Ontario)" said Reid. Go-betweens had to be arranged and it took two weeks of talking before someone—Harkness is probably the only man to know exactly who—arranged the drop. And that's why June Harkness found the Stanley Cup in her basement. As per their pact, she never asked about it. Wally said nothing.

There was just one remaining detail. The identity of either the thieves or the go-betweens had to be covered up. The public needed to be deceived on when the Cup was actually returned so all the parties involved had an alibi. And so Wally Harkness cooked one up. He told his friends at the paper that the Cup had been dropped off a couple of mornings after it had arrived on his doorstep. He said the family's black poodle Marcel had awakened him one morning and there, at the foot of his driveway, were the trophies. The newspapermen didn't ask too many questions and Wally allowed them a shot of himself and the hardware at police headquarters. "I feel like the Chief," said Wally, referring to Leafs' captain George Armstrong who had earned the Cup just three years earlier. That's where the picture on June's wall came from.

Ten years later, Wally had risen to the position of deputy chief but an old friend from the business world prevailed upon him to head security for his auto parts company and Wally said why not. A little while later, they found lymphoma in Wally. After extensive treatments, the doctors thought he had beaten it back. "I have wonderful news," June wrote friends, "it looks like Wally will be all right." But then the cancer came back and it galloped through his body. He died June 12, 1981. He was only forty-seven.

June thinks of Wally every day, probably every hour. "He's always on my mind," she says simply. And when she watches television, she only has to tilt her head the slightest degree to see the picture. The one of the Stanley Cup and the hero—her hero—who saved it.

Chapter 14

SILVER AND GOLD

Ken Morrow played 10 NHL seasons as a dependable defenseman and finished his career with 17 goals, a good month for Wayne Gretzky. Yet there is a convincing argument that Morrow, not Gretzky, nor Orr nor Maurice Richard, had a better season than the 1979-80 campaign, a year in which Morrow went goalless. In 1980, Morrow, now forty-two, was a member of the U.S. gold medal "Miracle on Ice" winners in Lake Placid. That spring, he held down a starting spot on the blue line as the Islanders won their first Stanley Cup. In one season, Morrow managed to garner the highest prize in hockey's amateur and professional arenas: an Olympic gold medal and a Stanley Cup.

Morrow, now the Islanders' Director of Professional Scouting and a resident of Kansas City, said comparing Olympic gold and Lord Stanley's silver is impossible. He holds his ground when pressed on which one he could be forced to surrender. "I wouldn't give up either," Morrow says. "Nationwide, I'm better remembered for the Olympics. In the New York area, it's for the Islanders. The gold medal is such a unique thing and it's something you keep. I sometimes take it in to show school kids and they get a real kick out of it. But the Stanley Cup is the best trophy around. When I see the gold football they give to the winner of the Super Bowl or the World Series trophy, I laugh. They look so hokey. The Stanley Cup is simple but elegant. It's irresistible, No matter where you take it people's eyes light up.

"I remember one year, I picked it up from (teammate) Steffan

Ken Morrow, Olympic gold medalist and Stanley Cup champion.
(Hockey Hall of Fame Archives)

Perrson's house and I just threw it in the back seat. I drove a little ways and then I saw the flashing lights behind me and I thought, 'Oh boy, here we go.' Sure enough, the cops pull me over, walk up to the car and point to the back seat. The one cop says, 'I thought that's what you had back there' and they spent the next little while looking at the names. I had a neighbor and every year I would let him borrow it for a couple of hours. He would take pictures of the Cup and himself, he would be laying in bed with it, having breakfast with it like the Cup was a person."

And while the Olympic gold medal remains the standard for excellence in amateur athletics, the Stanley Cup retains a more tangible value. "For the last couple of years when we were winning, I would take it to some bars and restaurants I knew around Long Island," Morrow said. "The owners would come up and get their pictures taken with it. I can't count the number of bars or restaurants there are in Long Island with a framed picture of the owner and the Stanley Cup. And I'll tell you, when you bring the Cup once into one of those places, you're set for life for a meal or a drink."

Denis Potvin. (author's collection)

Chapter 15

ONE FINAL SPRING

It was 1983, and while spring bloomed with promise in Edmonton, the portents of autumn were everywhere in Uniondale, Long Island.

The New York Islanders had won three consecutive Stanley Cups with a team that was both solid and spectacular. Up front, the ephemeral Mike Bossy supplied the fireworks. Resolute and gifted, center Bryan Trottier provided the grit and resolve. But the Islanders won from the blue line in—thanks to superb clutch goaltending from Billy Smith and intractable physical and positional play from the club's lifeblood, defenseman Denis Potvin.

Potvin had succeeded Bobby Orr as the Norris Trophy winner for best defenseman in 1976. He won it again in 1978 and 1979 and he, as much as anyone, exemplified the Islanders' way. Tremendously skilled, he was also rabidly competitive and in his prime he stood as the most versatile defenseman in the game, a player who could overrun an opponent with a winning goal or a savage body check.

But Denis Potvin was thirty in 1983 and the Islanders, whose dominance at the dawn of the decade seemed impregnable, were weakening. Time, like water lapping against stone, was eroding skills. Battles, while won, still scraped away layers of resolve. Fatigue, ignored in youth, weighted every step. While the Islanders remained immensely formidable, the idea was returning to the league that the team was, at long last, vulnerable. Their heirs were gathered in Edmonton, and they were named Gretzky, Kurri, Coffey, and Fuhr.

The Oilers served notice they were ready to assume the crown in 1983. Edmonton had 10 more points in the standings and scored a staggering total of 122 more goals. Wayne Gretzky had more assists, 125, than anyone else in the league had points. Four Oilers, Mark Messier, Gretzky, Jari Kurri, and Glenn Anderson stood among the league's top 10 scorers. Bossy was the only Islander to make the list.

Shadows were lengthening in Potvin's life away from the rink as well. His father, Armand, had cancer and even today as Denis Potvin speaks of his father, you sense a grief behind his eyes and hear a catch in his voice.

Armand Potvin was a small man but stocky and powerful. He played hockey with a terrific senior team in Perth, Ontario, the Blue Wings, and even earned an invitation to the training camp of the Detroit Red Wings. It was there he suffered a serious back injury that ended his playing career and disqualified him from service in the army. He was now an ex-athlete, and while he settled down comfortably in Ottawa as a civil servant, the inability to play wounded him. "There was a real void in his life from that," Denis Potvin said. "He really didn't skate again until the early 1950s when he started skating with us. There was nothing he liked more than to play hockey and there was no secret that having three boys gave him an opportunity to hope one of them would become a professional athlete."

All three did. Jean Potvin beat his brother to the NHL, but their father schooled all of his sons in the way of the athlete. "You really do play for your dad in most cases," Denis Potvin recalled. "He's the guy who shows you all along he has those expectations of you. Mom is very important, but in a different way. I am by no means belittling the role of Mom, but there was that association with Dad because he was there. When I played football and got hurt, he was always the first one on the field to say 'How are you doing, suck it up, you'll be fine.' There was always a feeling of invincibility that I got from him. He would say if you don't want to get hurt, you wouldn't. There was always the fear that I might hurt myself, but he taught me to play all the sports and to love them all."

Now, like brushfires that precede a fiery holocaust, cancer plagued the father who, to Potvin, had symbolized strength and invincibility. "He started out with lung cancer," Denis said. "It went from his lungs to the pancreas and he even had some in the head. I remember the doctors telling me, if they could figure out why a cancer moves from one part of the body to another, they would be so much further ahead. It's a mystery."

Before that 1982-83 season, Denis Potvin had struck an audacious deal with Armand. This Cup would be for him, as long as he promised to stay true to the treatments and ensure he would be on hand to see it won.

"My dad and I kept talking about how it was improbable that I could win but that I was going to give it all I had. He made the promise that he would do the same thing, that he would live through everything to see us bring home the Stanley Cup."

When they reached the finals that spring, the Islanders found the Oilers waiting but the champions, still skilled and tough, were not yet ready to fall. The Islanders beat Edmonton 2-0 in Game One and then stunned both Edmonton and the hockey world with a four-game sweep. Years later, the Oilers would point to that series as the one in which they learned what it took to be champions. They could barely believe their eyes when they saw the Islanders out of uniform after the game. The Stanley Cup winners were battered nearly beyond recognition, the splints and slings they eschewed to play were finally, grudgingly accepted. But they had won.

Sometime around 11:00 p.m. on the night of May 17, spring returned to Uniondale, New York, in the form of a 4-2 victory, a fourth consecutive Stanley Cup and a signal between a father and son. Denis Potvin—as captain, the first New York Islander to grasp the Stanley Cup—lifted it to the owner's box, where Armand Potvin stood and cheered beside Islanders' GM Bill Torrey.

After the postgame celebration in the dressing room, Potvin

scooped up the Cup and went home. "Dad was staying with me and I wanted to bring the Cup with me right away, because Dad had to go home for more treatments in Ottawa," Potvin said.

"We brought the Cup back home and it was a time in our living room, and I still have pictures of it, just my Dad, me, and the Stanley Cup. My wife and my mother just left Dad and me alone with the Cup." There was, in the ways of men, nothing and yet everything said. "There didn't have to be a lot said," Potvin recalled. "Dad talked about the beauty of it and how heavy it was and stuff like that. I think we talked a lot of gibberish, not wanting to deal with what was happening." They moved around, took pictures, looked at names, reminisced.

"We had this ottoman," Potvin said. "We sat in front of the ottoman and around the ottoman, always with the Stanley Cup next to Dad," Potvin said slowly. "I enjoyed the picture of my dad, finally, having the Cup. Then it was my turn, he and I, we kind of rotated around this ottoman and took some pictures. We danced for the first and only time in our lives that night, both of us moving around that ottoman. He was a good guy. The most sincere expressions, the touching that we did during that period of time, that was more important than words."

Not even the glow of the Stanley Cup would halt the cancer in Armand Potvin. The treatments to stop its spread left him partially blind and weak. "He couldn't see anymore and he couldn't talk," Denis remembered. "He eventually came out of it but there was a period of several months that were probably the most damaging. That therapy probably killed him, it took all his will to live away."

They came for Denis Potvin the following spring, when the Islanders were fighting for a fifth Stanley Cup against Washington. "We had pretty much taken over the series against Washington. My brother Jean was doing radio with the Islanders and he got the call that our dad had finally passed away. I decided to play that night; I couldn't figure anything else to do. So we played, I played kind of in a fog, sometimes I was there, and sometimes I wasn't. We won the game and I remember, I got off the ice and all these emotions were inside me. I guess there was anger involved and I wanted to get that out. On the way out, I started looking for a room. I didn't want to go back into the dressing room because I felt what was going to happen. I kept going, and there was nobody in this one room. I walked right into that room and closed the door and I sat down and I cried."

He cried there until his brother came for him. Remembering that night, tears roll down the face of the Islanders' hard rock Hall of Famer. "I remember playing later on but it felt like the buildings were empty now. I loved the game of hockey, but when he died, unquestionably it took my whole desire for the game away."

There would be no more Stanley Cups for Denis Potvin. The Islanders and the Oilers met again in the final the next year and after the two clubs split the first two games, Mark Messier scored a spectacular goal to give Edmonton the lead in Game 3. "They didn't look at us the same way anymore after that," Potvin said. "They didn't have that awe anymore and you could just feel the thing was slipping away from us. We couldn't get it back and they won three straight games."

The Islanders would never again return to the final. Armand Potvin was gone, too soon at sixty-three. Forestalled, winter could not be fended off. It was now someone else's turn and for Denis Potvin, winter had arrived.

But oh, what a fine autumn. The one that still produces a tear. The one with the old man, his son, the ottoman, and the Stanley Cup.

Chapter 16

WHO'S THE ROUND GUY WITH AL?

Al Braun has lived a life remarkably free of the sensational. He is a big man, six-foot-five, 240 pounds, who for nearly 20 years has worked in the auto body shop at an Edmonton, Alberta car dealership named Freedom Ford. He has two kids, a wife, and roots in Edmonton. He is a borderline sports fan but, like so many, he finds the ticket prices a stretch for a working family. "It'll cost you $200 for a night out," he says. "How many people can afford that?"

All that said, Al Braun has done something that only a small number of people in the world have done, something nearly every Canadian and a huge number of Americans, not to mention Russians, Swedes, and Finns would pay dearly to do. And Al has the picture to prove it.

One day, in the spring of 1988, Al was pounding out a fender when the owner of his business, a man named Jerry Fraser approached him. His boss said he had a very special job. Behind Fraser stood Lyle Kulchisky, the veteran trainer of the Edmonton Oilers. He was holding the Stanley Cup and it looked bad. It was dented, it was soggy with beer, and the ebony plate on which it was mounted was noticeably scratched.

The Oilers had won it a couple of nights before and had brought it to the people. The Cup was unchaperoned in those days and ever the sport, it had incurred extracurricular wear and tear. The dealership had seasons tickets for the Oilers and had once been owned by the club's owner, Peter Pocklington, so when Kulchisky needed fast repair work, he tried there.

"We had to do it really fast," Braun said. "Lyle said they had to get it looking better in time for the team picture. The first thing we had to do was straighten it up," Braun said. "I seem to remember it had been in the bottom of someone's swimming pool. The barrel was dented and there was beer all over it. There were two or three guys and we jumped right into it."

And so three employees of an Edmonton body shop set about repairing the most venerable sporting trophy in North America. Braun was the lead man. He figured out how the ebony plate came apart from the frame and piece-by-piece, the Cup was disassembled. The painter polished the rings and applied black paint to touch up the base while Braun worked to restore the rings. By lunchtime, looking resplendent, the Stanley Cup was handed back to Kulchisky but first, just so the grandkids would believe the story, the men of the body shop posed with their prize.

The Oilers, for the record, reject the notion they were particularly rough on the Cup. "The Cup was falling apart when we got it," said Edmonton publicity director Bill Tuele. "We took better care of it than most teams."

There is a moral in all this. At Freedom Ford, as at any place of business, you pay for the work they do. The Cup job was a freebie; even, if you like, a civic duty. No charge means no payment for the men who worked on it. Al Braun lost a morning's pay, maybe $100 bucks in 1988 dollars. "Ah, the guy was in a spot, you help him out," said Braun. "What goes around comes around."

And this is how it has. Sometimes, Braun will have guests over to the basement of his house and, naturally enough, hockey talk ensues. And that's when Al Braun tells the story. Invariably, his guests disbelieve him and with a chagrined countenance, he points to the wall, and to the picture of him and the Stanley Cup.

It is, he figures, the best value for $100 he will ever see.

Chapter 17

THE MANHATTAN TRANSFER

When the New York Rangers won the Stanley Cup in 1994, they set a new standard for celebration. It had been, after all, 54 years since the Cup had last been won by the Rangers and the editors of *Sports Illustrated* dispatched a reporter to monitor the Cup's goings-on.

The magazine reported that five hours after captain Mark Messier skated the Cup around Madison Square Garden, the Cup was taken to a Manhattan saloon named the Auction House. Among the luminaries swigging champagne from the bowl that night were tennis star John McEnroe, actor Tim Robbins, and longtime Ranger star Rod Gilbert. When the bartenders ran out of Cristal champagne, they switched to Dom Perignon and then, finally, Budweiser. Ranger Esa Tikkanen emptied the Cup and brought it outside the bar to 89th street. "This trophy isn't for the players," Tikkanen said, "it's for you, the good people of New York."

Two days later, the Cup was with defenseman Sergei Zubov at Restaurant National, a Russian nightclub in Brooklyn. "We not fill the Cup with borscht," said manager Simon Maklin. "Nobody touch him. When Rangers eat, I take him away from stage and put him inside office. When we want to make a picture, I take him out." The next day, the Cup rode up Broadway in a ticker tape parade. Afterwards a cop named Jim Jones put the Cup in his squad car, belted it in and delivered it to its next assignment. Six days after the victory, the champagne was still

The New York Rangers. (Doug MacLellan / Hockey Hall of Fame Archives)

flowing. Rangers' defenseman Nick Kypreos and star defense-
man Bryan Leetch brought the Cup to a bar named the China
Club. Among the group photographed with the Cup was San
Francisco 49er star Jerry Rice and actress Brooke Shields.

Kypreos, Mark Messier, and Leetch brought the Cup to
Columbia-Presbyterian Hospital where they dropped in on
Brian Buluver, a thirteen-year-old awaiting a heart transplant.
"When Brian saw the Cup, he smiled for the first time in seven
weeks," said his father Bill. "He was too weak to speak, yet I'd
never seen him so happy."

That night, the New York Yankees issued a press credential
for Stanley Cup and the trio of Rangers carried it through the
Yankees' clubhouse. A few minutes later, the Cup sat in the dugout
as Messier, in Yankee pinstripes, caught pitcher Steve Howe in
the bullpen. The Cup was carried to George Steinbrenner's box.
With 27,000 fans chanting "Let's Go Rangers" and pointing to
the Cup, the Yankees beat Minnesota 6-4.

Ranger Ed Olczyk brought the Cup to visit a friend who
worked the till at a tobacco shop near the Rangers' practice rink
in Rye, New York. Olczyk had called a few days before and left

a cryptic message: "On Friday, remember to bring your camera. I'm going to have a little surprise for you."

When Olczyk arrived at the store, 400 people were waiting for him. "I'm so sorry," Olczyk's friend said, "I only told one person." Later, Olczyk filled the bowl with feed and let Kentucky Derby winner Go for Gin use it as a feedbag at Belmont Park Racetrack.

Ranger equipment trainer Joe Murphy brought the Cup to the Providence Rest Nursing Home in the Bronx. The nuns running the home set it on a pedestal and swathed it in blue velvet. "The Cup is not the Holy Grail," said home operator Sister Joanne—who, of course, would know—"but it is very, very special."

Chapter 18

STANLEY C. RILEY

Karma, reincarnation, spiritual intervention, none of these things comes with certificates of authenticity. You have three choices: you believe, you don't believe, or you wonder. This is the story of two people who wonder and one little boy who will.

By 1997, Cheryl Riley had long resigned herself to the fact that she would never have children. She had spent 17 years trying to conceive but doctors told her the chances of being able to bear a child were remote. In 1954, her mother took the drug DES to prevent miscarriages. Years later, her mother was sitting in a doctor's waiting room when she noticed an article on DES in a copy of *Reader's Digest*.

DES, widely prescribed in the 1950s, was found to sometimes cause devastating damage to the reproductive systems of female fetuses. Cheryl was sixteen when her mother found the article. She submitted herself to a battery of tests. Doctors told her the damage had been substantial but there was a remote chance she could conceive. As she grew into adulthood, she used birth control but she gave that up in 1980 when she met a gentle carpenter named Ken Riley. The two married in 1982 and after several years of trying to conceive, she was reexamined. Again the doctors concluded there was but a remote chance of conception. The two considered and then rejected the remaining medical options. In-vitro fertilization seemed invasive and would be terribly expensive. In the end, they settled for what they had, a full life with friends and their children.

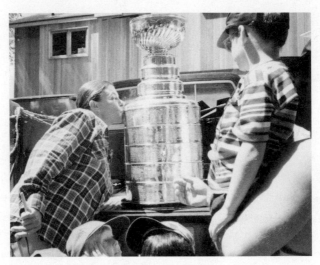

Cheryl Riley's fateful kiss. (The Riley Family)

"We considered adoption," said Ken, 'but we knew how complicated it was and how much was involved. We just decided to leave things as they were." Still, there was a quiet, sometimes sharp grief over the thought neither would be parents.

"We both love kids but we had resigned ourselves to the fact that it wasn't going to happen," Cheryl said. "I know in the back of my mind, I regretted it. I was green with envy with some of my girlfriends, but I had accepted it. I was close to the children of a lot of my friends."

And then, in August of 1996, the Stanley Cup came into their lives. Mike Ricci, then a member of the Colorado Avalanche, owned a cottage near Wilberforce. Ricci invited a few friends, including Ken's boss for a look at the newly won Cup. Naturally enough, several hundred people showed up, including Ken, a hockey fan, and Cheryl, a good sport. Ken asked the Cup chaperone whether he could touch the Cup. Cheryl impulsively asked whether she could kiss it. "I kiss things that I hold dear," she said. "I don't really know why I did it, just to say I did, I guess." After a few pictures with the Cup and some socializing, the two went home. That night or the next...Shazam! Cheryl became

Cheryl and Ken Riley with Stanley C. Riley. (The Riley Family)

pregnant. "I don't actually know if it was that night," Cheryl said, "but I do know it was that weekend."

At first, Cheryl couldn't believe she was pregnant. "I hadn't taken any birth control for 17 years," she said, "when suddenly I was feeling very funny." The doctors were staggered. In view of her medical history and age—Cheryl was forty-two—they proceeded cautiously. Cheryl had eight ultrasounds and an amniocentesis. After a 30-hour labor, Stanley arrived. This is where the wondering comes about.

"If the Stanley Cup hadn't come and I hadn't kissed it, I might never have become pregnant," Cheryl said. "I believe heavily in things that maybe don't make sense. I believe in karma. I do believe in spirits and in reincarnation."

"I've thought about it a lot," said Ken, "and all I can say is that it's pretty weird. Some things are just hard to know."

There had been no decision on the child's name prior to the birth, but a friend had suggested Stanley, in view of the circumstances of the conception, and the idea grew on Ken. When her son was born, Cheryl heard Ken say: "All right, Stan my man." You had to admit it fit. The boy was christened Stanley C.

Gordon Jeff Riley. They refrained from giving him the middle name "Cup" and settled on the middle initial "C" for "Cup," instead. "He's going to have enough explaining to do as it is," Cheryl said. "How many little boys do you know named Cup?"

Ken has taught his son to recognize Gordie Howe on a calendar and Stan's small toy stick was so common around the house, it seemed to grow out of his hand. He loves to watch his father play old-timers' hockey and nothing delights little Stanley more than playing hockey. Around two years old, he began shutting the bathroom and bedroom doors. That served as the signal for one of his parents that little Stanley needed a goal. They blocked off the doorway to their kitchen with a turned-over coffee table. Then, on the family's hardwood floors, Stanley grabs his stick and aims a ball at a tiny net in front of the kitchen doorway, practicing his shot.

Ken and Cheryl told Stanley's story to a local reporter. She wrote an article that found its way to the research and resource area of Toronto's Hockey Hall of Fame. A newspaper reporter, in the Hall for research, spied it and eventually brought Stanley's story across Canada on the 32-member Southam Newspaper chain. Suddenly, Stanley was a celebrity. A Wilberforce man, sitting in his daughter's Vancouver home, had just listened to her harangue that nothing worth noting happened back home. He opened the morning paper, saw the story about Stanley, and grinned broadly before, paper in hand, launching his rebuttal.

The postmaster in Wilberforce still makes a big fuss over Stanley as the town's celebrity, whenever he sees Cheryl and her son at the grocery store. Cheryl has a scrapbook of the articles about Stanley.

Ricci himself heard of his part in the story. "Actually, I've seen the little guy around the lake a few times," he said. "He's a great kid. I'm very happy for them."

Stanley will be an only child, "No hope for a Connie Smythe," said Cheryl who feels amply blessed with one miracle.

Chapter 19

THE HEAVIEST TROPHY

It's several hours before the game at Toronto's Air Canada Centre. Slava Fetisov pulls off a New Jersey Devils' warm-up jacket and tosses aside a sweat-laden shirt. He is drenched.

Even as an assistant coach with the Devils, Fetisov exudes the same work ethic that made him one of the most remarkable players to lace up skates. Most assistant coaches cruise through a pregame skate. Fetisov whips his body, an athlete even in postplayer repose. This is a man who keenly understands work, responsibility, and burdens. And yet when he thinks of the Stanley Cup, the first thing he mentions is the trophy's weight. "It's heavy," Fetisov said. "Heavy in many, many ways."

Until he won two Stanley Cups in his final two years in the National Hockey League, Viacheslav (Slava) Fetisov had earned everything but what, to him, had come to matter most. Those Stanley Cup wins, in 1997 as a member of the vaunted Russian Five unit and the one in 1998, without wounded Wing Vladimir Konstantinov, were the crowning moments of a career hockey analysts say rivaled that of any defender, including Montreal great Doug Harvey, Denis Potvin, and even the legendary Bobby Orr.

Wayne Gretzky said Fetisov in his prime was the toughest defenseman to beat one-on-one he had ever faced. "No one saw the ice the way Fetisov did," said longtime Canadiens' rearguard Larry Robinson. Fetisov won nine World Championships, many as captain, and always as the linchpin, of the devastating

The Cup in Moscow's Red Square (Hockey Hall of Fame Archives)

Soviet Union National Team.

And yet, for all his gifts, Fetisov's life has been one of often-unbearable tragedy.

A few days after his first Cup win, Fetisov was in the limousine that smashed into a tree in a Detroit suburb, an accident in which he sustained serious leg injuries. He was the luckiest. Konstantinov, the most dominant Detroit defenseman since Black Jack Stewart ruled the Red Wings' blue line in the 1940s, as well as Red Wings' trainer Sergei Manatsakanov, suffered profound and disabling head injuries.

Fetisov's on-ice greatness didn't stop Soviet officials from throwing him off the team for voicing his desire to play in North America in the late 1980s. As a young man, he lost his brother in a car accident that came with Fetisov at the wheel. He endured five often-frustrating seasons with the New Jersey Devils in which he never completely adapted to the NHL style of play and was traded to the Red Wings. In the kind of vicious turns of fate that has marked Fetisov's life and career, the Red Wings advanced to the finals and fell to the Devils, his old

Fetisov in the Red WIngs' locker room. (Hockey Hall of Fame Archives)

team, in four straight games.

And then on June 7, 1997, a few moments after the Wings swept aside the Philadelphia Flyers, captain Steve Yzerman accepted the Cup from commissioner Gary Bettman and motioned for Fetisov. Typically, Fetisov declined to arrive alone, just the way he would not defect from the Soviet Union for fear of reprisals toward his family and teammates. Fetisov signaled to center Igor Larionov. "We went through a lot together, Igor and I, and opened gates for Russians." Fetisov said. "I called Igor and said let's go. It was probably one of my most memorable moments ever, to skate around the ice and hold the Cup."

How far he had come. In his first years in the NHL, a Russian was viewed as an outsider who had come, in the eyes of some, to steal North American jobs. Fetisov was run at and taunted nightly in his first years with the Devils. In the Stanley Cup he found the perfect symbol of acceptance. The honor of receiving the trophy from the captain, ahead of MVP goalie Mike Vernon and a host of players who had more Red Wings seniority, was a tangible sign that finally, the great Fetisov was being given his due.

"It meant respect for me," Fetisov said. "Steve is a classy guy. People on the team maybe did more than I did but we went through a lot to fight and to be in this situation. It was unforgettable."

Thirty-nine-year-old Viacheslav Fetisov, at that moment the oldest player in the NHL, had come further than anyone. He first auditioned for the Red Army program as a six-year-old and earned a spot in the club's development system at eight. From the start, he studied the game and at a young age understood its rhythms in the way of the prodigy. With the Soviet National Team, Fetisov was a member of what is often referred to as the best five-man unit ever to grace a rink. Alexei Kasatonov joined him on the blue line and the KLM line, Larionov, Vladimir Krutov, and Sergei Makarov at forward. The line raced through World Championships and Olympic games, Fetisov won two Olympic golds, and the unit shredded NHL talent in their infrequent exhibitions.

Fetisov flowered as the rarest of players, someone who could turn the game's flow to his own purposes. Fetisov was bestowed the Order of Lenin, the highest award a Soviet Citizen could garner. He was the undisputed leader of the best hockey team in the world and yet, he was profoundly unhappy. He had seen how the system discarded aged and injured players and knew, someday, his fate would be the same. "When you were done, they threw you out," he has said. "You had nothing and you died alone. I didn't want that to be me."

There were medical issues as well. Fetisov and his wife Lada had been unable to conceive, and a move to North America would mean a chance at more advanced technology and perhaps, the chance to have a child. The reaction from Soviet officials was swift and punitive. He was suspended from the Red Army team and threatened with detention to Siberia. He was banned from every rink in Russia. The great Fetisov managed to practice in a rink owned by a pencil factory. He was browbeaten by generals. "They screamed like crazy men," Fetisov said. "They couldn't believe anyone would refuse to follow their order. That instant, I was terrified. One instant is all they needed to turn you from a hero to the enemy. I knew they could destroy me."

He was told the only way he could get his release from the army was to get written approval from three dozen military officials. He went door to door, often spending five days to get one signature. But the Captain in the Red Army would not relent and, fearing reprisals against family and friends he would leave behind, would not defect. The players voted as a block not to play in the 1989 World Championships without their captain. Fetisov was reinstated, the Soviets won the World Championship, and Fetisov was named tournament MVP. Finally in May of 1989, during the giddy early days of perestroika, Fetisov was allowed to come and go as he pleased, provided his new employer, the New Jersey Devils, forked over a healthy release fee.

But the player who arrived on U.S. soil with the Devils was not the same one who had dominated the European game. He was tired from the battles, baffled by the language and the often-artless style of play in the NHL. "I had fought a powerful system," Fetisov said. "I was unprepared for the pressure and I didn't have the energy to fight any more." Fetisov never scored more than eight goals or accrued more than 42 points. Alexei Kasatnov, who had not backed Fetisov in his battle with the Soviet authorities, was also imported onto the Devils' blue line. Fetisov saw that as a betrayal and the two barely communicated.

Fetisov played five seasons with the Devils, and then was traded to the Red Wings for a third-round draft choice, a ludicrously low return for a player of his caliber. He played 14 regular season games with the Wings and witnessed their colossal disappointment in the 1996 final against his old team, New Jersey.

But Red Wings' coach Scotty Bowman, long an admirer, had a plan. With Konstantinov and Fetisov on the blue line, he used Larionov at center and Vyacheslav Kozlov and Sergei Fedorov, normally a center, on the wing. They were the Russian Five and their assigned positions meant little. Thanks to their common background and training methods, they weaved and switched positions effortlessly. It was as if a piece of the old Soviet hockey machine had been grafted onto an NHL team and the acknowledged ringmaster was Fetisov.

And then came that night in June of 1997. The Red Wings beat the Flyers 2-1. Fetisov's long journey had brought him to the hockey player's ultimate destination.

"For some reason I didn't want to see the Cup before that night," Fetisov said. "It didn't belong to me. Suddenly Steve handed it to me, and it's heavy. I couldn't believe it. I couldn't find my wife and she was with me for so long and supported me through difficult situations in my life. We finally met and stayed a long time together in the dressing room. It was the most memorable time in my life. I received so many awards, gold medals, and I stood on the Olympic pedestal, but this thing has so much history, it's heavy."

Fetisov organized a trip to Russia with the Cup and the luster took on even greater dimension in its touchdown on Russian soil. "I didn't know what it would be like in Moscow." Fetisov said. "I knew they televised the Stanley Cup final in Russia the last few years. I knew the Red Wings had a lot of fans in Russia because of the Russian Five. But the reaction was incredible. From people in Russia, ordinary fans to the Prime Minister and President Yeltsin, everyone wanted to see the Cup." Fetisov's ascendancy to the title of Stanley Cup champion and the reaction to the Cup in Russia helped lay to rest one of the enduring myths about Russian hockey players, that they didn't have a cultural background that revered the Cup and would not, therefore, render the sacrifices necessary to win it.

"If you're going to think the Stanley Cup is cultural, you're wrong," said Viacheslav Fetisov. "The National Hockey League is the most international league in the world. If you bring the Cup to Japan, they're going to have the same reaction.

"This Cup has so much positive energy, it's incredible. People can feel this when they hold the Cup."

POSTSCRIPT

This book hasn't unearthed every Stanley Cup story; no one book could, for this trophy's stories are as thick as the carpet of signatures nicked into the original bowl.

Instead, consider this book a flashlight shining into a cavernous library. There are thousands of other stories in the past and thousands being written every year as the Cup accrues new admirers daily.

Maybe the weight of those stories is the heaviness felt by Slava Fetisov when he lifted the Stanley Cup. Bobby Clarke felt it light. The weight, it seems, depends on the burdens of the man bearing the Cup and the rigors of the road to claim it.

That road is being walked every day, on the ice or in the gym or in the mind of a child who, for the first time, sees the Stanley Cup. Every book about Stanley, including this one, is "to be continued..."

CUP NAMES

Stanley Cup winners, according to the NHL's Guide and Record Book

Name	Team	Year
Clarence Abel	New York Rangers	1928
	Chicago Black Hawks	1934
Sid Abel	Detroit Red Wings	1943, 1950, 1952
Douglas Acer	Montreal Victorias	1899
Keith Acton	Edmonton Oilers	1988
Jack Adams	Toronto Arenas	1918
	Ottawa Senators	1927
Andy Aikenhead	New York Rangers	1933
Tommy Albelin	New Jersey Devils	1995
"Bones" Allen	Ottawa Silver Seven	1905
Keith Allen	Detroit Red Wings	1954
Glenn Anderson	Edmonton Oilers	1984, 1985, 1987, 1988, 1990
	New York Rangers	1994
Jocko Anderson	Victoria Cougars	1925
Lloyd Andrews	Toronto St Pats	1922
Syl Apps	Toronto Maple Leafs	1942, 1947, 1948
Al Arbour	Detroit Red Wings	1954
	Chicago Black Hawks	1961
	Toronto Maple Leafs	1962, 1963, 1964
Jack Armitage	Winnipeg Victorias	1896
George Armstrong	Toronto Maple Leafs	1962
Josh Arnold	Montreal Wanderers	1906
Barry Ashbee	Philadelphia Flyers	1974
Arthur Asmundson	New York Rangers	1933
Larry Aurie	Detroit Red Wings	1937
Ralph Backstrom	Montreal Canadiens	1959, 1960, 1965, 1966, 1968, 1969
Garnet "Ace" Bailey	Boston Bruins	1972
Irvine "Ace" Bailey	Toronto Maple Leafs	1932
Dan Bain	Winnipeg Victorias	1896, 1901, 1902
Earl Balfour	Chicago Black Hawks	1961
Dave Balon	Montreal Canadiens	1965, 1966
Bill Barber	Philadelphia Flyers	1974, 1975

Bill Barilko	Toronto Maple Leafs	1947, 1948, 1949, 1951
Billy Barlow	Montreal AAA	1893, 1894
Tom Barrasso	Pittsburgh Penguins	1991, 1992
Marty Barry	Detroit Red Wings	1936, 1937
Bobby Bauer	Boston Bruins	1939, 1941
Bobby Baun	Toronto Maple Leafs	1962, 1963, 1964, 1967
Roxi Beaudro	Kenora Thistles	1906
Ed Belfour	Dallas Stars	1999
Jean Beliveau	Montreal Canadiens	1956, 1957, 1958, 1959, 1960, 1965, 1966, 1968, 1969, 1971
Billy Bell	Montreal Canadiens	1924
Billy Bellingham	Montreal AAA	1902, 1903
Brian Bellows	Montreal Canadiens	1993
Clint Benedict	Ottawa Senators	1920, 1921, 1923
	Montreal Maroons	1926
Max Bentley	Toronto Maple Leafs	1948, 1949, 1951
Red Berenson	Montreal Canadiens	1965
Lois Berlinguette	Montreal Canadiens	1916
Jeff Beukeboom	Edmonton Oilers	1987, 1988, 1990
	New York Rangers	1994
Cecil Blachford	Montreal AAA	1903
	Montreal Wanderers	1906, 1907, 1908, 1910
Tom Bladon	Philadelphia Flyers	1974, 1975
Andy Blair	Toronto Maple Leafs	1932
Toe Blake	Montreal Maroons	1935
	Montreal Canadiens	1944, 1946
Russ Blinko	Montreal Maroons	1935
Gus Bodnar	Toronto Maple Leafs	1945, 1947
Garth Boesch	Toronto Maple Leafs	1947, 1948, 1949
Serge Boisvert	Montreal Canadiens	1986
Hugh Bolton	Toronto Maple Leafs	1951
Marcel Bonin	Detroit Red Wings	1955
	Montreal Canadiens	1958, 1959, 1960
Dickie Boon	Montreal AAA	1902, 1903
Christian Bordeleau	Montreal Canadiens	1986
Mike Bossy	New York Islanders	1980, 1981, 1982, 1983
Butch Bouchard	Montreal Canadiens	1944, 1946, 1953, 1956
Pierre Bouchard	Montreal Canadiens	1971, 1973, 1976, 1977, 1978
Billy Boucher	Montreal Canadiens	1924
Bobby Boucher	Montreal Canadiens	1924
Frank Boucher	New York Rangers	1928, 1933
George Boucher	Ottawa Senators	1920, 1921, 1923, 1927
Leon Bourgault	New York Rangers	1928

Bob Bourne	New York Islanders	1980, 1981, 1982, 1983
Phil Bourque	Pittsburgh Penguins	1991, 1992
Paul Boutilier	New York Islanders	1983
Johnny Bower	Toronto Maple Leafs	1962, 1963, 1964, 1967
Russell Bowie	Montreal Victorias	1899
Ralph Bowman	Detroit Red Wings	1936, 1937
Bill Boyd	New York Rangers	1928
Jack Brannen	Montreal Shamrocks	1899, 1900
Doug Brennan	New York Rangers	1933
Carl Brewer	Toronto Maple Leafs	1962, 1963, 1964
Frank Brimsek	Boston Bruins	1939, 1941
Patrice Brisebois	Montreal Canadiens	1993
Harry Broadbent	Ottawa Senators	1920, 1921, 1923
	Montreal Maroons	1926
Turk Broda	Toronto Maple Leafs	1942, 1947, 1948, 1949, 1951
Connie Broden	Montreal Canadiens	1957
Martin Brodeur	New Jersey Devils	1995
Bernie Brophy	Montreal Maroons	1926
Neal Broten	New Jersey Devils	1995
Connie Brown	Detroit Red Wings	1943
Dave Brown	Edmonton Oilers	1990
Doug Brown	Detroit Red Wings	1997, 1998
G. Brown	Winnipeg Victorias	1901, 1902
Morley Bruce	Ottawa Senators	1920, 1921
Benoit Brunet	Montreal Canadiens	1993
Mud Bruneteau	Detroit Red Wings	1936, 1937, 1941
Sergei Brylin	New Jersey Devils	1995
Kelly Buchberger	Edmonton Oilers	1990
Johnny Bucyk	Boston Bruins	1970, 1972
Marty Burke	Montreal Canadiens	1930, 1931
F. Cadham	Winnipeg Victorias	1902
Herb Cain	Montreal Maroons	1935
	Boston Bruins	1941
Jock Callander	Pittsburgh Penguins	1992
Patsy Callighen	New York Rangers	1928
Allan Cameron	Montreal AAA	1893, 1894
Billy Cameron	Montreal Canadiens	1924
Harry Cameron	Toronto Blue Shirts	1914
	Toronto Arenas	1918
	Toronto St Pats	1922
C.J. "Tote" Campbell	Winnipeg Victorias	1896
Guy Carbonneau	Montreal Canadiens	1986, 1993
	Dallas Stars	1999
Wayne Carleton	Boston Bruins	1970
Bobby Carpenter	New Jersey Devils	1995
Lorne Carr	Toronto Maple Leafs	1942, 1945
Billy Carroll	New York Islanders	1981, 1982, 1983
	Edmonton Oilers	1985
Bill Carson	Boston Bruins	1929

Frank Carson	Montreal Maroons	1926
Gerald Carson	Montreal Canadiens	1930
Joe Carveth	Detroit Red Wings	1943
Wayne Cashman	Boston Bruins	1970, 1972
Jay Caufield	Pittsburgh Penguins	1991, 1992
Lorne Chabot	New York Rangers	1928
	Toronto Maple Leafs	1932
Murph Chamberlain	Montreal Canadiens	1944 1946
Shawn Chambers	New Jersey Devils	1995
	Dallas Stars	1999
Rick Chartraw	Montreal Canadiens	1976, 1977, 1978, 1979
Gerry Cheevers	Boston Bruins	1970, 1972
Chris Chelios	Montreal Canadiens	1986
Tom Chorske	New Jersey Devils	1995
Jeff Chychrun	Pittsburgh Penguins	1992
Francis "King" Clancy	Ottawa Senators	1923, 1927
	Toronto Maple Leafs	1932
Aubrey "Dit" Clapper	Boston Bruins	1929, 1939, 1941
Bobby Clarke	Philadelphia Flyers	1974, 1975
Odie Cleghorn	Montreal Canadiens	1924
Sprague Cleghorn	Ottawa Senators	1920, 1921
	Montreal Canadiens	1924
Bill Clement	Philadelphia Flyers	1974, 1975
Paul Coffey	Edmonton Oilers	1984, 1985, 1987
	Pittsburgh Penguins	1991
Danton Cole	New Jersey Devils	1995
Herbert Collins	Montreal AAA	1894
Mac Colville	New York Rangers	1940
Neil Colville	New York Rangers	1940
Brian Conacher	Toronto Maple Leafs	1967
Charlie Conacher	Toronto Maple Leafs	1932
Lionel Conacher	Chicago Black Hawks	1934
	Montreal Maroons	1935
Pat Conacher	Edmonton Oilers	1984
Roy Conacher	Boston Bruins	1939, 1941
Alex Connell	Ottawa Senators	1927
	Montreal Maroons	1935
Bert Connolly	Chicago Black Hawks	1938
Cam Connor	Montreal Canadiens	1979
Bill Cook	New York Rangers	1928, 1933
Fred "Bun" Cook	New York Rangers	1928, 1933
Lloyd Cook	Vancouver Millionaires	1915
Tom Cook	Chicago Black Hawks	1934
Bert Corbeau	Montreal Canadiens	1916
Con Corbeau	Toronto Blue Shirts	1914
Rene Corbet	Colorado Avalanche	1996
Les Costello	Toronto Maple Leafs	1948
Hal Cotton	Toronto Maple Leafs	1932
Jack Coughlin	Toronto Arenas	1918
Art Coulter	Chicago Black Hawks	1934
	New York Rangers	1940

Yvan Cournoyer	Montreal Canadiens	1965, 1966, 1968, 1969, 1971, 1973, 1977, 1978, 1979
Geoff Courtnall	Edmonton Oilers	1988
Billy Couture	Montreal Canadiens	1924
Rosie Couture	Chicago Black Hawks	1934
Bruce Cowick	Philadelphia Flyers	1974
Bill Cowley	Boston Bruins	1939, 1941
Jack Crawford	Boston Bruins	1939, 1941
Russell Crawford	Quebec Bulldogs	1913
Rusty Crawford	Toronto Arenas	1918
Billy Creighton	Quebec Bulldogs	1913
Terry Crisp	Philadelphia Flyers	1974, 1975
Alex Currie	Ottawa Senators	1911
Floyd Curry	Montreal Canadiens	1953, 1956, 1957, 1958
Kjell Dahlin	Montreal Canadiens	1986
Cully Dahlstorm	Chicago Black Hawks	1938
J.J. Daigneault	Montreal Canadiens	1993
Vincent Damphousse	Montreal Canadiens	1993
Mathieu Dandenault	Detroit Red Wings	1997, 1998
Ken Daneyko	New Jersey Devils	1995
Jeff Daniels	Pittsburgh Penguins	1993
Hal Darragh	Toronto Maple Leafs	1932
Jack Darragh	Ottawa Senators	1911, 1920, 1921, 1923
Alan Davidson	Toronto Blue Shirts	1914
Bob Davidson	Toronto Maple Leafs	1942, 1945
Cam Davidson	Montreal Victorias	1896, 1897, 1898
Shirley Davidson	Montreal Victorias	1895, 1896, 1897
Lorne Davis	Montreal Canadiens	1953
Bob Dawes	Toronto Maple Leafs	1949
Hap Day	Toronto Maple Leafs	1932
Adam Deadmarsh	Colorado Avalanche	1996
Kevin Dean	New Jersey Devils	1995
Alex Delvecchio	Detroit Red Wings	1952, 1954, 1955
Corb Denneny	Toronto Arenas	1918
	Toronto St Pats	1922
Cy Denneny	Ottawa Senators	1920, 1921, 1923, 1927
	Boston Bruins	1929
Eric Desjardins	Montreal Canadiens	1993
Al Dewbury	Detroit Red Wings	1950
Edgar Dey	Ottawa Senators	1909
Ernie Dickens	Toronto Maple Leafs	1942
Cecil Dillon	New York Rangers	1933
Bill Dineen	Detroit Red Wings	1954, 1955
Chuck Dinsmore	Montreal Maroons	1926
Dion (no first name)	Ottawa Silver Seven	1906
Gilbert Dionne	Montreal Canadiens	1993
Paul DiPietro	Montreal Canadiens	1993
Gary Doak	Boston Bruins	1970

John Dobby	Montreal Shamrocks	1899
Kent Douglas	Toronto Maple Leafs	1963
Les Douglas	Detroit Red Wings	1943
Jim Dowd	New Jersey Devils	1995
Kris Draper	Detroit Red Wings	1997, 1998
Gordie Drillon	Toronto Maple Leafs	1942
Graham Drinkwater	Montreal Victorias	1895, 1896, 1897, 1898, 1899
Bruce Driver	New Jersey Devils	1995
Dick Duff	Toronto Maple Leafs	1962, 1963
	Montreal Canadiens	1965, 1966
Donald Dufresne	Montreal Canadiens	1993
Woody Dumart	Boston Bruins	1939, 1941
Andre "Moose" Dupont	Philadelphia Flyers	1974, 1975
Bill Durnan	Montreal Canadiens	1944, 1946
Babe Dye	Toronto St Pats	1922
Ebbs (no first name)	Ottawa Silver Seven	1906
Frank Eddolls	Montreal Canadiens	1946
Gerry Ehman	Toronto Maple Leafs	1964
Roland Elliot	Montreal Victorias	1895
	Montreal AAA	1902
Ron Ellis	Toronto Maple Leafs	1967
Wally Elmer	Victoria Cougars	1925
Brian Engblom	Montreal Canadiens	1977, 1978, 1979
Aut Erickson	Toronto Maple Leafs	1967
Anders Ericsson	Detroit Red Wings	1998
Bob Errey	Pittsburgh Penguins	1991, 1992
Phil Esposito	Boston Bruins	1970, 1972
Tony Esposito	Montreal Canadiens	1969
Jack Evans	Chicago Black Hawks	1961
Stewart Evans	Montreal Maroons	1935
Todd Ewen	Montreal Canadiens	1993
Jack Ewing	Montreal Victorias	1897, 1898, 1899
Bill Ezinicki	Toronto Maple Leafs	1947, 1948, 1949
Art Farrell	Montreal Shamrocks	1899, 1900
Sergei Fedorov	Detroit Red Wings	1997, 1998
Jim Fenwick	Montreal Victorias	1895
John Ferguson	Montreal Canadiens	1965, 1966, 1968, 1969, 1971
Viacheslav Fetisov	Detroit Red Wings	1997, 1998
Bob Fillion	Montreal Canadiens	1944, 1946
Dave Finnie	Ottawa Silver Seven	1905
Frank Finnigan	Ottawa Senators	1927
	Toronto Maple Leafs	1932
Stephane Fiset	Colorado Avalanche	1996
Joe Fisher	Detroit Red Wings	1943
Fern Flaman	Toronto Maple Leafs	1951
Reggie Fleming	Chicago Black Hawks	1961
Bill Flett	Philadelphia Flyers	1974
Magnus Flett	Winnipeg Victorias	1901, 1902
Rod Flett	Winnipeg Victorias	1896, 1901, 1902
Theoren Fleury	Calgary Flames	1989

Lee Fogolin (Jr.)	Edmonton Oilers	1984, 1985
Lee Fogolin (Sr.)	Detroit Red Wings	1950
Adam Foote	Colorado Avalanche	1996
Peter Forsberg	Colorado Avalanche	1996
Charles Fortier	Montreal Canadiens	1924
Jaques Fournier	Montreal Canadiens	1916
Frank Foyston	Toronto Blue Shirts	1914
	Victoria Cougars	1925
Ron Francis	Pittsburgh Penguins	1991, 1992
Jimmy Franks	Detroit Red Wings	1937
A.A. Fraser	Ottawa Silver Seven	1903
George Fraser	Victoria Cougars	1925
Frank Fredrickson	Victoria Cougars	1925
	Boston Bruins	1929
Grant Fuhr	Edmonton Oilers	1984, 1985, 1987, 1988, 1990
Johnny Gagnon	Montreal Canadiens	1931
Bob Gainey	Montreal Canadiens	1976, 1977, 1978, 1979, 1986
Dutch Gainor	Boston Bruins	1929
Perk Galbraith	Boston Bruins	1929
John Gallagher	Detroit Red Wings	1937
Bruce Gamble	Toronto Maple Leafs	1967
Dick Gamble	Montreal Canadiens	1953
Chuck Gardiner	Chicago Black Hawks	1934
Cal Gardner	Toronto Maple Leafs	1949, 1951
Jim Gardner	Montreal AAA	1902, 1903
	Montreal Wanderers	1910
Horace Gaul	Ottawa Silver Seven	1905
	Ottawa Senators	1911
Jean Gauthier	Montreal Canadiens	1965
George Gee	Detroit Red Wings	1950
Martin Gelinas	Edmonton Oilers	1990
Bernie Geoffrion	Montreal Canadiens	1953, 1956, 1957, 1958, 1959, 1960
Eddie Gerard	Ottawa Senators	1920, 1921, 1923
	Toronto St Pats	1922
Eddie Geroux	Kenora Thistles	1907
Ray Getliffe	Boston Bruins	1939
	Montreal Canadiens	1944
Greg Gilbert	New York Islanders	1982, 1983
	New York Rangers	1994
Brent Gilchrist	Detroit Red Wings	1998
	New York Islanders	1980, 1981, 1982, 1983
Randy Gilhen	Pittsburgh Penguins	1991
Clark Gillies	New York Islanders	1980, 1981, 1982, 1983
David Gillilan	Montreal Victorias	1896, 1897
Billy Gilmour	Ottawa Silver Seven	1903, 1904, 1905, 1906
	Ottawa Senators	1909

Dave Gilmour	Ottawa Silver Seven	1903
Doug Gilmour	Calgary Flames	1989
Larry Gilmour	Montreal Wanderers	1908
S.C. "Suddy" Gilmour	Ottawa Silver Seven	1903, 1904
A.B. "Tony" Gingras	Winnipeg Victorias	1901, 1902
Gaston Gingras	Montreal Canadiens	1986
Frank "Pud" Glass	Montreal Wanderers	1906, 1907, 1908, 1910
Bob Goldham	Toronto Maple Leafs	1942, 1947
	Detroit Red Wings	1952, 1954, 1955
Leroy Goldsworthy	Chicago Black Hawks	1934
Hank Goldup	Toronto Maple Leafs	1942
Larry Goodenough	Philadelphia Flyers	1975
Eddie Goodfellow	Detroit Red Wings	1936, 1937
Paul Goodman	Chicago Black Hawks	1938
Butch Goring	New York Islanders	1980, 1981, 1982, 1983
Ed Gorman	Ottawa Senators	1927
Johnny Gottselig	Chicago Black Hawks	1934, 1938
Phil Goyette	Montreal Canadiens	1956, 1957, 1958, 1959, 1960
Bob Gracie	Toronto Maple Leafs	1932
	Montreal Maroons	1935
Leith Graham	Ottawa Senators	1921
Danny Grant	Montreal Canadiens	1968
Mike Grant	Montreal Victorias	1895, 1896, 1897, 1898, 1899
Adam Graves	Edmonton Oilers	1990
	New York Rangers	1994
Alex Gray	New York Rangers	1928
Red Green	Boston Bruins	1929
Rick Green	Montreal Canadiens	1986
Randy Gregg	Edmonton Oilers	1984, 1985, 1987, 1988, 1990
Lucien Grenier	Montreal Canadiens	1969
Wayne Gretzky	Edmonton Oilers	1984, 1985, 1987, 1988
Si Griffis	Kenora Thistles	1907
	Vancouver Millionaires	1915
Don Grosso	Detroit Red Wings	1943
Bill Guerin	New Jersey Devils	1995
Alexei Gusarov	Colorado Avalanche	1996
Billy Hague	Ottawa Silver Seven	1906
George Hainsworth	Montreal Canadiens	1930, 1931
Harold Halderson	Victoria Cougars	1925
Glenn Hall	Chicago Black Hawks	1961
Joe Hall	Quebec Bulldogs	1912, 1913
Kevin Haller	Montreal Canadiens	1993
Milt Halliday	Ottawa Senators	1927
Mats Hallin	New York Islanders	1983
Red Hamil	Boston Bruins	1939
Reg Hamilton	Toronto Maple Leafs	1945

Dave Hannan	Edmonton Oilers	1988
	Colorado Avalanche	1996
Glen Harmon	Montreal Canadiens	1944, 1946
Terry Harper	Montreal Canadiens	1965, 1966, 1968, 1969, 1971
Bill Harris	Toronto Maple Leafs	1962, 1963, 1964
Ted Harris	Montreal Canadiens	1965, 1966, 1968, 1969
	Philadelphia Flyers	1975
Harriston (no first name)	Toronto Blue Shirts	1914
Wilf Hart	Victoria Cougars	1925
Mike Hartman	New York Rangers	1994
Doug Harvey	Montreal Canadiens	1953, 1956, 1957, 1958, 1959, 1960
Bob Hassard	Toronto Maple Leafs	1951
Derian Hatcher	Dallas Stars	1999
Bill Hay	Chicago Black Hawks	1961
Jim Hay	Detroit Red Wings	1955
Chris Hayes	Boston Bruins	1972
Glenn Healy	New York Rangers	1994
Sammy Hebert	Toronto Arenas	1918
Jerry Heffernan	Montreal Canadiens	1944
Ott Heller	New York Rangers	1933, 1940
Harry Helman	Ottawa Senators	1923
Harold Henderson	Montreal Victorias	1895, 1896, 1897
Lorne Henning	New York Islanders	1980, 1981
Riley Hern	Montreal Wanderers	1907, 1908, 1910
Bryan Hextall	New York Rangers	1940
Bill Hicke	Montreal Canadiens	1959, 1960
Wayne Hicks	Chicago Black Hawks	1961
Fred Higgengbotham	Winnepeg Victorias	1896
Mel Hill	Boston Bruins	1939, 1941
	Toronto Maple Leafs	1945
Sean Hill	Montreal Canadiens	1993
Dutch Hiller	New York Rangers	1940
	Montreal Canadiens	1946
Randy Hiller	Pittsburgh Penguins	1991
Larry Hillman	Detroit Red Wings	1955
	Toronto Maple Leafs	1962, 1963, 1964, 1967
	Montreal Canadiens	1969
Lionel Hitchman	Ottawa Senators	1923
	Boston Bruins	1929
Charlie Hodge	Montreal Canadiens	1959, 1960, 1965, 1966
Ken Hodge	Boston Bruins	1970, 1972
Tom Hodge	Montreal AAA	1902, 1903
Archie Hodson	Montreal AAA	1893, 1894
Kevin Hodson	Detroit Red Wings	1998
Charles Hoerner	Montreal Shamrocks	1899
Benoit Hogue	Dallas Stars	1999
Bobby Holik	New Jersey Devils	1995

Flash Hollett	Boston Bruins	1939, 1941
Harry Holmes	Toronto Blue Shirts	1914
	Toronto Arenas	1918
	Victoria Cougars	1925
Nicolas Holmstrom	Detroit Red Wings	1997, 1998
Albert Holway	Montreal Maroons	1926
Archie Hooper	Montreal AAA	1902
Art Hooper	Montreal AAA	1903
Tom Hooper	Kenora Thistles	1906
	Montreal Wanderers	1908
George Horne	Montreal Maroons	1926
Red Horner	Toronto Maple Leafs	1932
Tim Horton	Toronto Maple Leafs	1962, 1963, 1964, 1967
Rejean Houle	Montreal Canadiens	1971, 1973, 1977, 1978, 1979
H. Howard	Winnipeg Victorias	1896
Garry Howatt	New York Islanders	1980, 1981
Gordie Howe	Detroit Red Wings	1950, 1952, 1954, 1955
Syd Howe	Detroit Red Wings	1936, 1937, 1943
Jiri Hrdina	Calgary Flames	1989
	Pittsburgh Penguins	1991, 1992
Tony Hrkac	Dallas Stars	1999
Charlie Huddy	Edmonton Oilers	1984, 1985, 1987, 1988, 1990
Mike Hudson	New York Rangers	1994
Pat Hughes	Montreal Canadiens	1979
	Edmonton Oilers	1984, 1985
Bobby Hull	Chicago Black Hawks	1961
Brett Hull	Dallas Stars	1999
Dave Hunter	Edmonton Oilers	1984, 1985, 1987
Mark Hunter	Calgary Flames	1989
Tim Hunter	Calgary Flames	1989
J.B. "Bouse" Hutton	Ottawa Silver Seven	1903, 1904
Harry Hyland	Montreal Wanderers	1910
Alex Irving	Montreal AAA	1894
Art Jackson	Boston Bruins	1941
	Toronto Maple Leafs	1945
Busher Jackson	Toronto Maple Leafs	1932
Don Jackson	Edmonton Oilers	1984, 1985
Hal Jackson	Chicago Black Hawks	1938
	Detroit Red Wings	1943
Stan Jackson	Toronto St Pats	1922
Jaromir Jagr	Pittsburgh Penguins	1991, 1992
George James	Montreal Canadiens	1894
Doug Jarvis	Montreal Canadiens	1976, 1977, 1978, 1979
Larry Jeffries	Toronto Maple Leafs	1967
Roger Jenkins	Chicago Black Hawks	1934, 1938
Grant Jennings	Pittsburgh Penguins	1991, 1992
Ernie "Moose" Johnson	Montreal Wanderers	1906, 1907, 1908, 1910

Ivan "Ching" Johnson	New York Rangers	1928, 1933
Tom Johnson	Montreal Canadiens	1953, 1956, 1957, 1958, 1959, 1960
Virgil Johnson	Chicago Black Hawks	1938
Ed Johnston	Boston Bruins	1970, 1972
Charles W. Johnstone	Winnipeg Victorias	1896, 1901, 1902
Aurel Joliat	Montreal Canadiens	1924, 1930, 1931
Robert Jones	Montreal Victorias	1895, 1896
Tomas Jonsson	New York Islanders	1982, 1983
Bill Juzda	Toronto Maple Leafs	1949, 1951
Anders Kallur	New York Islanders	1980, 1981, 1982, 1983
Valeri Kamenski	Colorado Avalanche	1996
Bingo Kampman	Toronto Maple Leafs	1942
Mike Karakas	Chicago Black Hawks	1938
Alexander Karpovtsev	New York Rangers	1994
Mike Keane	Montreal Canadiens	1993
	Colorado Avalanche	1996
	Dallas Stars	1999
Butch Keeling	New York Rangers	1933
Bob Kelly	Philadelphia Flyers	1974, 1975
Pete Kelly	Detroit Red Wings	1936, 1937
Red Kelly	Detroit Red Wings	1950, 1952, 1954, 1955
	Toronto Maple Leafs	1962, 1963, 1964, 1967
Bill Kendall	Chicago Black Hawks	1934
Rod Kennedy	Montreal Wanderers	1906
Ted Kennedy	Toronto Maple Leafs	1945, 1947, 1948, 1949, 1951
Dave Keon	Toronto Maple Leafs	1962, 1963, 1964, 1967
Albert "Dubby" Kerr	Ottawa Senators	1909, 1911
Dave Kerr	New York Rangers	1940
Hec Kilrea	Ottawa Senators	1927
Wally Kilrea	Detroit Red Wings	1936, 1937
Orest Kindrachuk	Philadelphia Flyers	1974, 1975
A.P. Kingan	Montreal AAA	1893,1894
Hobie Kitchen	Montreal Maroons	1926
Lloyd Klein	Boston Bruins	1929
Jon Klemm	Colorado Avalanche	1996
Petr Klima	Edmonton Oilers	1990
Joe Klukay	Toronto Maple Leafs	1947, 1948, 1949, 1951
Mike Knuble	Detroit Red Wings	1998
Joe Kocur	New York Rangers	1994
	Detroit Red Wings	1997, 1998
Vladimir Konstantinov	Detroit Red Wings	1997
John Kordic	Montreal Canadiens	1986
Alexei Kovalev	New York Rangers	1994
Vyacheslav Kozlov	Detroit Red Wings	1997, 1998
Uwe Krupp	Colorado Avalanche	1996

Mike Krushelnyski	Edmonton Oilers	1985, 1987, 1988
Jari Kurri	Edmonton Oilers	1984, 1985, 1987, 1988, 1990
Tom Kurvers	Montreal Canadiens	1986
Nick Kypreos	New York Rangers	1994
Elmer Lach	Montreal Canadiens	1944, 1946, 1953
Normand Lacombe	Edmonton Oilers	1988
Guy Lafleur	Montreal Canadiens	1973, 1976, 1977, 1978, 1979
Fred Lake	Ottawa Senators	1909, 1911
Newsy Lalonde	Montreal Canadiens	1916
Mike Lalor	Montreal Canadiens	1986
Mark Lamb	Edmonton Oilers	1990
Yvon Lambert	Montreal Canadiens	1976, 1977, 1978, 1979
Leo Lamoureux	Montreal Canadiens	1944, 1946
Gord Lane	New York Islanders	1980, 1981, 1982, 1983
Myles Lane	Boston Bruins	1929
Pete Langelle	Toronto Maple Leafs	1942
Jamie Langenbrunner	Dallas Stars	1999
Dave Langevin	New York Islanders	1980, 1981, 1982, 1983
Albert Langlois	Montreal Canadiens	1958, 1959, 1960
Rod Langway	Montreal Canadiens	1979
Jacques Laperriere	Montreal Canadiens	1965, 1966, 1968, 1969, 1971, 1973
Guy Lapointe	Montreal Canadiens	1971, 1973, 1976, 1977, 1978,1979
Martin Lapointe	Detroit Red Wings	1997, 1998
Igor Larionov	Detroit Red Wings	1997, 1998
Steve Larmer	New York Rangers	1994
Wildor Larochelle	Montreal Canadiens	1930, 1931
Michel "Bunny" Larocque	Montreal Canadiens	1976, 1977, 1978, 1979
Claude Larose	Montreal Canadiens	1965, 1966, 1968, 1971, 1973
Pierre Larouche	Montreal Canadiens	1979
Jack Laviolette	Montreal Canadiens	1916
Jamie Leach	Pittsburgh Penguins	1992
Reg Leach	Philadelphia Flyers	1975
Stephan Lebeau	Montreal Canadiens	1993
Jackie LeClair	Montreal Canadiens	1956
John LeClair	Montreal Canadiens	1993
Albert Leduc	Montreal Canadiens	1930, 1931
Gary Leeman	Montreal Canadiens	1993
Brian Leetch	New York Rangers	1994
Sylvain Lefebvre	Colorado Avalanche	1996
Chuck Lefley	Montreal Canadiens	1971, 1973
Hughie Lehman	Vancouver Millionaires	1915
Jere Lehtinen	Dallas Stars	1999
Jacques Lemaire	Montreal Canadiens	1968, 1969, 1971

		1973, 1976, 1977, 1978, 1979
Moe Lemay	Edmonton Oilers	1987
Claude Lemieux	Montreal Canadiens	1986
	New Jersey Devils	1995
	Colorado Avalanche	1996
Mario Lemieux	Pittsburgh Penguins	1991, 1992
George Leonard	Quebec Bulldogs	1912
Pit Lepine	Montreal Canadiens	1930, 1931
Curtis Leschyshyn	Colorado Avalanche	1996
Art Lesieur	Montreal Canadiens	1931
Percy LeSueur	Ottawa Silver Seven	1906
	Ottawa Senators	1909, 1911
Bill Lesuk	Boston Bruins	1990
Tony Leswick	Detroit Red Wings	1952, 1954, 1955
Alex Levinsky	Toronto Maple Leafs	1932
	Chicago Black Hawks	1938
Danny Lewicki	Toronto Maple Leafs	1951
Gordon Lewis	Montreal Victorias	1897, 1898, 1899
Herbie Lewis	Detroit Red Wings	1936, 1937
Doug Lidster	New York Rangers	1994
Nicklas Lidstrom	Detroit Red Wings	1997, 1998
Charles Liffiton	Montreal AAA	1902, 1903
	Montreal Wanderers	1908
Ted Lindsay	Detroit Red Wings	1950, 1952, 1954, 1955
Willy Lindstrom	Edmonton Oilers	1984, 1985
Ken Linseman	Edmonton Oilers	1984
Carl Liscombe	Detroit Red Wings	1943
Ed Litzenberger	Chicago Black Hawks	1961
	Toronto Maple Leafs	1962, 1963, 1964
Troy Loney	Pittsburgh Penguins	1991, 1992
Ross Lonsberry	Philadelphia Flyers	1974, 1975
Hakan Loob	Calgary Flames	1989
Jim Lorentz	Boston Bruins	1970
Bob Lorimer	New York Islanders	1980, 1981
Clem Loughlin	Victoria Cougars	1925
G.S. Lowe	Montreal AAA	1893
Kevin Lowe	Edmonton Oilers	1984, 1985, 1987, 1988, 1990
	New York Rangers	1994
Craig Ludwig	Montreal Canadiens	1986
	Dallas Stars	1999
Dave Lumley	Edmonton Oilers	1984, 1985
Harry Lumley	Detroit Red Wings	1950
Gilles Lupien	Montreal Canadiens	1978, 1979
Vic Lynn	Toronto Maple Leafs	1947, 1948, 1949
Kilby Macdonald	New York Rangers	1940
Al MacInnis	Calgary Flames	1989
Mickey MacKay	Vancouver Millionaires	1915
	Boston Bruins	1929
Fleming Mackell	Toronto Maple Leafs	1949, 1951

Howard Mackie	Detroit Red Wings	1937
John MacLean	New Jersey Devils	1995
Rick MacLeishh	Philadelphia Flyers	1974, 1975
Brian MacLellan	Calgary Flames	1989
John MacMillan	Toronto Maple Leafs	1962, 1963
Jamie Macoun	Calgary Flames	1989
	Detroit Red Wings	1997, 1998
Craig MacTavish	Edmonton Oilers	1987, 1988, 1990
	New York Rangers	1994
Frank Mahovlich	Toronto Maple Leafs	1962, 1963, 1964, 1967
	Montreal Canadiens	1971, 1973
Peter Mahovlich	Montreal Canadiens	1971, 1973, 1976, 1977
Fernand Majeau	Montreal Canadiens	1944
Chico Maki	Chicago Black Hawks	1961
David Maley	Montreal Canadiens	1986
Kenny Mallen	Vancouver Millionaires	1915
Jeff Malone	Quebec Bulldogs	1913
Joe Malone	Quebec Bulldogs	1912, 1913
	Montreal Canadiens	1924
Kirk Maltby	Detroit Red Wings	1997, 1998
George Mantha	Montreal Canadiens	1930, 1931
Sylvio Mantha	Montreal Canadiens	1924, 1930, 1931
Milan Marcetta	Toronto Maple Leafs	1967
Don Marcotte	Boston Bruins	1970, 1982
Hector Marini	New York Islanders	1981, 1982
Gus Marker	Montreal Maroons	1935
Jack Marks	Quebec Bulldogs	1912, 1913
	Toronto Arenas	1918
Harold "Mush" Marsh	Chicago Black Hawks	1934, 1938
Don Marshall	Montreal Canadiens	1956, 1957, 1958, 1959, 1960
Grant Marshall	Dallas Stars	1999
Jack Marshall	Winnipeg Victorias	1901
	Montreal AAA	1902, 1903
	Montreal Wanderers	1907, 1910
	Toronto Blue Shirts	1914
Clare Martin	Detroit Red Wings	1950
Paul Masnick	Montreal Canadiens	1953
Stephane Matteau	New York Rangers	1994
Richard Matvichuk	Dallas Stars	1999
Jean Matz	Vancouver Millionaires	1915
Ed Mazur	Montreal Canadiens	1953
Al McAdam	Philadelphia Flyers	1974
Chris McAlpine	New Jersey Devils	1995
Bert McCaffrey	Montreal Canadiens	1930, 1931
Darren McCarty	Detroit Red Wings	1997, 1998
Kevin McClelland	Edmonton Oilers	1984, 1985, 1987, 1988
Frank McCool	Toronto Maple Leafs	1945
Johnny McCormack	Toronto Maple Leafs	1951

	Montreal Canadiens	1953
Johnny McCreedy	Toronto Maple Leafs	1942, 1945
Brad McCrimmon	Calgary Flames	1989
Ab McDonald	Montreal Canadiens	1959, 1960
	Chicago Black Hawks	1961
Bucko McDonald	Detroit Red Wings	1936, 1937
	Toronto Maple Leafs	1942
Jack McDonald	Quebec Bulldogs	1912
Lanny McDonald	Calgary Flames	1989
A. McDougall	Montreal Victorias	1895
Bob McDougall	Montreal Victorias	1895, 1897,1898
Hartland McDougall	Montreal Victorias	1895, 1896, 1897, 1898
Shawn McEachern	Pittsburgh Penguins	1992
Mike McEwen	New York Islanders	1981, 1982, 1983
Jim McFadden	Detroit Red Wings	1950
Don McFayden	Chicago Black Hawks	1934
Frank McGee	Ottawa Silver Seven	1903, 1904, 1905, 1906
Jim McGee	Ottawa Silver Seven	1904
F. "Roy" Mc Giffen	Toronto Blue Shirts	1914
Billy McGimsie	Kenora Thistles	1906
Randy McKay	New Jersey Devils	1995
Jack McKell	Ottawa Senators	1920, 1921
Alex McKendry	New York Islanders	1980
Jim McKenna	Montreal Shamrocks	1899
Joe McKenna	Montreal Shamrocks	1900
Don McKenney	Toronto Maple Leafs	1964
Bill McKenzie	Chicago Black Hawks	1938
John McKenzie	Boston Bruins	1970, 1972
Ernie McLea	Montreal Victorias	1896, 1897, 1898, 1899
Jack McLean	Toronto Maple Leafs	1945
Mike McMahon	Montreal Canadiens	1944
Sammy McManus	Montreal Maroons	1935
George McNamara	Toronto Blue Shirts	1914
Howard McNamara	Montreal Canadiens	1916
Gerry McNeil	Montreal Canadiens	1953, 1957, 1958
Mike McPhee	Montreal Canadiens	1986
Bud McPherson	Montreal Canadiens	1953
Pat McReavy	Boston Bruins	1941
Fred McRobie	Montreal Victorias	1899
Marty McSorley	Edmonton Oilers	1987, 1988
Howie Meeker	Toronto Maple Leafs	1947, 1948, 1949, 1951
Harry Meeking	Toronto Arenas	1918
	Victoria Cougars	1925
Roland Melanson	New York Islanders	1981, 1982, 1983
Larry Melnyk	Edmonton Oilers	1985
Henri Menard	Montreal Wanderers	1906
Wayne Merrick	New York Islanders	1980, 1981, 1982, 1983
Horace Merrill	Ottawa Senators	1920

G.H. Merritt	Winnipeg Victorias	1896
Mark Messier	Edmonton Oilers	1984, 1985, 1987, 1988, 1990
	New York Rangers	1994
Don Metz	Toronto Maple Leafs	1942, 1945, 1947, 1948, 1949
Nick Metz	Toronto Maple Leafs	1942, 1945, 1947, 1948
Dave Michayluk	Pittsburgh Pengins	1992
Stan Mikita	Chicago Black Hawks	1961
Bill Miller	Montreal Maroons	1935
Earl Miller	Toronto Maple Leafs	1932
Joe Miller	New York Rangers	1928
Dimitri Mironov	Detroit Red Wings	1998
Nolan Mitchell	Toronto St Pats	1922
Mike Modano	Dallas Stars	1999
Percy Molson	Montreal Victorias	1897
Armand Mondou	Montreal Canadiens	1930, 1931
Pierre Mondou	Montreal Canadiens	1977, 1978, 1979
Andy Moog	Edmonton Oilers	1984, 1985, 1987
Alf Moore	Chicago Black Hawks	1938
Arthur Moore	Ottawa Silver Seven	1903, 1904, 1905, 1906
Dickie Moore	Montreal Canadiens	1953, 1956, 1957, 1958, 1959, 1960
Paddy Moran	Quebec Bulldogs	1912, 1913
Howie Morenz	Montreal Canadiens	1924, 1930, 1931
Elwyn Morris	Toronto Maple Leafs	1945
Ken Morrow	New York Islanders	1980, 1981, 1982, 1983
Gus Mortson	Toronto Maple Leafs	1947, 1948, 1949, 1951
Ken Mosdell	Montreal Canadiens	1946, 1953, 1956
Alex Motter	Detroit Red Wings	1943
Johnny Mowers	Detroit Red Wings	1943
Joe Mullen	Calgary Flames	1989
	Pittsburgh Penguins	1991, 1992
Kirk Muller	Montreal Canadiens	1993
Harry Mummery	Quebec Bulldogs	1913
	Toronto Arenas	1918
Craig Muni	Edmonton Oilers	1987, 1988, 1990
Dunc Munro	Montreal Maroons	1926
Bob Murdoch	Montreal Canadiens	1971, 1973
Murray Murdoch	New York Rangers	1928, 1933
Joe Murphy	Edmonton Oilers	1990
Larry Murphy	Pittsburgh Penguins	1991, 1992
	Detroit Red Wings	1997, 1998
Ron Murphy	Chicago Black Hawks	1961
Troy Murray	Colorado Avalanche	1996
Dana Murzyn	Calgary Flames	1989
Clare Mussen	Montreal AAA	1894
Mark Napier	Montreal Canadiens	1979

	Edmonton Oilers	1985
Mats Naslund	Montreal Canadiens	1986
Ric Nattress	Calgary Flames	1989
Mike Needham	Pittsburgh Penguins	1992
Sergei Nemchinov	New York Rangers	1994
Eric Nesterneko	Chicago Black Hawks	1961
Bob Nevin	Toronto Maple Leafs	1962, 1963
Billy Nicholson	Montreal AAA	1902, 1903
Scott Niedermayer	New Jersey Devils	1995
Joe Nieuwendyk	Calgary Flames	1989
	Dallas Stars	1999
Frank Nighbor	Vancouver Millionaires	1915
	Ottawa Senators	1920, 1921,1923, 1927
Chris Nilan	Montreal Canadiens	1986
Kent Nilsson	Edmonton Oilers	1987
Reg Noble	Toronto Arenas	1918
	Toronto St Pats	1922
	Montreal Maroons	1926
Simon Nolet	Philadelphia Flyers	1974
Brian Noonan	New York Rangers	1935
Bill Nyrop	Montreal Canadiens	1976, 1977, 1978
Bob Nystrom	New York Islanders	1980, 1981, 1982, 1983
Eddie Oatman	Quebec Bulldogs	1912
Buddy O'Connor	Montreal Canadiens	1944, 1946
Lyle Odelein	Montreal Canadiens	1993
Ed Olczyk	New York Rangers	1994
Harry Oliver	Boston Bruins	1929
Bert Olmstead	Montreal Canadiens	1953, 1956, 1957, 1958
	Toronto Maple Leafs	1962
Tom "Windy" O'Neill	Toronto Maple Leafs	1945
Jimmy Orlando	Detroit Red Wings	1943
Bobby Orr	Boston Bruins	1970, 1972
Chris Osgood	Detroit Red Wings	1997, 1998
Joel Otto	Calgary Flames	1989
George Owen	Boston Bruins	1929
Sandis Ozolinsh	Colorado Avalanche	1996
Jim Paek	Pittsburgh Penguins	1991, 1992
Pete Palangio	Chicago Black Hawks	1938
Jim Pappin	Toronto Maple Leafs	1964, 1967
Bernie Parent	Philadelphia Flyers	1974, 1975
Tom Paton	Montreal AAA	1893
Frank Patrick	Vancouver Millionaires	1915
Lester Patrick	Montreal Wanderers	1907
Lynn Patrick	New York Rangers	1940
Muzz Patrick	New York Rangers	1940
Colin Patterson	Calgary Flames	1989
Marty Pavelich	Detroit Red Wings	1950, 1952, 1954, 1955
Barry Pederson	Pittsburgh Penguins	1991

Mike Peluso	New Jersey Devils	1995
Jim Peplinski	Calgary Flames	1989
Steffan Persson	New York Islanders	1980, 1981, 1982, 1983
Garry Peters	Boston Bruins	1972
Jimmy Peters	Montreal Canadiens	1946
	Detroit Red Wings	1950, 1954
Eric Pettinger	Boston Bruins	1929
Gord Pettinger	New York Rangers	1933
	Detroit Red Wings	1936, 1937
	Boston Bruins	1939
Bill Phillips	Montreal Maroons	1926
Tom Phillips	Montreal AAA	1903
	Kenora Thistles	1907
Noel Picard	Montreal Canadiens	1965
Frank Pieterangelo	Pittsburgh Penguins	1992
Alf Pike	New York Rangers	1940
Pierre Pilote	Chicago Black Hawks	1961
Didier Pitre	Montreal Canadiens	1916
Gerry Plamondon	Montreal Canadiens	1946
Derek Plante	Dallas Stars	1999
Jacques Plante	Montreal Canadiens	1953, 1956, 1957, 1958, 1959, 1960
Michel Plasse	Montreal Canadiens	1973
Bud Poile	Toronto Maple Leafs	1947
Mike Polich	Montreal Canadiens	1977
Jack Portland	Boston Bruins	1939
Denis Potvin	New York Islanders	1980, 1981, 1982, 1983
Jean Potvin	New York Islanders	1980
Georges Poulin	Montreal Canadiens	1916
Jaroslav Pouzar	Edmonton Oilers	1984, 1985, 1987
"Rocket" Power	Quebec Bulldogs	1913
Babe Pratt	New York Rangers	1940
	Toronto Maple Leafs	1945
Price (no first name)	Ottawa Senators	1920
Noel Price	Montreal Canadiens	1966
Ken Priestlay	Pittsburgh Penguins	1992
Joe Primeau	Toronto Maple Leafs	1932
Goldie Prodgers	Quebec Bulldogs	1912
	Montreal Canadiens	1916
Andre Pronovost	Montreal Canadiens	1958, 1959, 1960
Claude Pronovost	Montreal Canadiens	1956, 1957, 1958, 1959, 1960, 1965, 1966, 1968, 1969
Marcel Pronovost	Detroit Red Wings	1950, 1952, 1954, 1955
	Toronto Maple Leafs	1967
Claude Provost	Montreal Canadiens	1956, 1957, 1958, 1959, 1960, 1965, 1966
Metro Prystai	Detroit Red Wings	1952, 1954

Bob Pulford	Toronto Maple Leafs	1962, 1963, 1964, 1967
Harvey Pulford	Ottawa Silver Seven	1903, 1904, 1905, 1906
William Pullan	Montreal Victorias	1895
Jamie Pushor	Detroit Red Wings	1997
Jean Pusie	Montreal Canadiens	1931
Andre Racicot	Montreal Canadiens	1993
Rob Ramage	Calgary Flames	1989
	Montreal Canadiens	1993
Ken Randall	Toronto Arenas	1918
	Toronto St Pats	1922
Bill Ranford	Edmonton Oilers	1988, 1990
Norman Rankin	Montreal Victorias	1895
Ken Reardon	Montreal Canadiens	1946
Terry Reardon	Boston Bruins	1941
Billy Reay	Montreal Canadiens	1946, 1953
Eldon "Pokey" Reddick	Edmonton Oilers	1990
Mickey Redmond	Montreal Canadiens	1968, 1969
Earl Reibel	Detroit Red Wings	1954, 1955
Dave Reid	Dallas Stars	1999
Leo Reise	Detroit Red Wings	1950, 1952
Glenn "Chico" Resch	New York Islanders	1980
Mike Ricci	Colorado Avalanche	1996
Henri Richard	Montreal Canadiens	1956, 1957, 1958, 1959, 1960, 1965, 1966, 1968, 1969, 1971, 1973
Maurice Richard	Montreal Canadiens	1944, 1946, 1953, 1956, 1957, 1958, 1959
Frank Richardson	Montreal Victorias	1898, 1899
Stephane Richer	Montreal Canadiens	1986
	New Jersey Devils	1995
Mike Richter	New York Rangers	1994
Bruce Ridpath	Ottawa Senators	1911
Doug Riseborough	Montreal Canadiens	1976, 1977, 1978, 1979
Gus Rivers	Montreal Canadiens	1930, 1931
John Ross Roach	Toronto St Pats	1922
Mario Roberge	Montreal Canadiens	1993
Phil Roberto	Montreal Canadiens	1971
Gary Roberts	Calgary Flames	1989
Gord Roberts	Pittsburgh Penguins	1991, 1992
Jim Roberts	Montreal Canadiens	1965, 1966, 1973, 1976, 1977
Earl Robertson	Detroit Red Wings	1937
Fred Robertson	Toronto Maple Leafs	1932
Earl Robinson	Montreal Maroons	1935
Larry Robinson	Montreal Canadiens	1973, 1976, 1977, 1978, 1979, 1986
Leon Rochefort	Montreal Canadiens	1966

Ernie Rodden	Boston Bruins	1929
Al Rollins	Toronto Maple Leafs	1951
Brian Rolston	New Jersey Devils	1995
Doc Romnes	Chicago Black Hawks	1934, 1938
Ed Ronan	Montreal Canadiens	1993
Skene Ronan	Montreal Canadiens	1916
Steve Rooney	Montreal Canadiens	1986
Walter Rooney	Quebec Bulldogs	1912
Art Ross	Kenora Thistles	1907
	Montreal Canadiens	1908
Sam Rothschield	Montreal Maroons	1926
Bob Rouse	Detroit Red Wings	1997, 1998
Bobby Rousseau	Montreal Canadiens	1965, 1966, 1968, 1969
Haviland Routh	Montreal AAA	1893, 1894
Patrick Roy	Montreal Canadiens	1986, 1993
	Colorado Avalanche	1996
Reijo Ruotsalainen	Edmonton Oilers	1987, 19990
Ernie Russell	Montreal Wanderers	1906, 1907, 1908, 1910
Warren Rychel	Colorado Avalanche	1996
Joe Sakic	Colorado Avalanche	1996
Don Saleski	Philadelphia Flyers	1974, 1975
Phil Samis	Toronto Maple Leafs	1948
Kjell Samuelsson	Pittsburgh Penguins	1992
Ulf Samuelsson	Pittsburgh Penguins	1991, 1992
Derek Sanderson	Boston Bruins	1970, 1972
Denis Savard	Montreal Canadiens	1993
Serge Savard	Montreal Canadiens	1968, 1969, 1973, 1976, 1977, 1978, 1979
Terry Sawchuk	Detroit Red Wings	1952, 1954, 1955
	Toronto Maple Leafs	1967
Fred Scanlon	Montreal Shamrocks	1899, 1900, 1902
Milt Schmidt	Boston Bruins	1939, 1941
Mathieu Schneider	Montreal Canadiens	1993
Dan Schock	Boston Bruins	1970
Sweeney Schriner	Toronto Maple Leafs	1942, 1945
Dave Schultz	Philadelphia Flyers	1974, 1975
Scott (no first name)	Ottawa Silver Seven	1904
Jim Seaborn	Vancouver Millionaires	1915
Earl Seibert	New York Rangers	1933
	Chicago Black Hawks	1938
Dave Semenko	Edmonton Oilers	1984, 1985
Richard Sevigny	Montreal Canadiens	1979
Eddie Shack	Toronto Maple Leafs	1962, 1963, 1964, 1967
Brendan Shanahan	Detroit Red Wings	1997, 1998
Bobby Sheehan	Montreal Canadiens	1971
Allan Sheilds	Montreal Maroons	1935
Johnny Sheppard	Chicago Black Hawks	1934
John Sherf	Detroit Red Wings	1937

Alex Shibicky	New York Rangers	1940
Jack Shill	Chicago Black Hawks	1938
Eddie Shore	Boston Bruins	1929, 1939
Hamby Shore	Ottawa Silver Seven	1905
	Ottawa Senators	1911
Steve Shutt	Montreal Canadiens	1973, 1976, 1977, 1978, 1979
Albert "Babe" Siebert	Montreal Maroons	1926
	New York Rangers	1933
Jon Sim	Dallas Stars	1999
Don Simmons	Toronto Maple Leafs	1962, 1963
Cully Simon	Detroit Red Wings	1943
Craig Simpson	Edmonton Oilers	1988, 1990
P.T. "Percy" Sims	Ottawa Silver Seven	1903
Alf Skinner	Toronto Arenas	1918
Glen Skov	Detroit Red Wings	1952, 1954, 1955
Brian Skrudland	Montreal Canadiens	1986
	Dallas Stars	1999
Blake Sloan	Dallas Stars	1999
Tod Sloan	Toronto Maple Leafs	1949, 1951
	Chicago Black Hawks	1961
Walter Small	Montreal Wanderers	1907
Alex Smith	Ottawa Senators	1927
Alf Smith	Ottawa Silver Seven	1904, 1905, 1906
Billy Smith	New York Islanders	1980, 1981, 1982, 1983
Bobby Smith	Montreal Canadiens	1986
Clint Smith	New York Rangers	1940
Dallas Smith	Boston Bruins	1970, 1972
Des Smith	Boston Bruins	1941
Geoff Smith	Edmonton Oilers	1990
George Smith	Montreal AAA	1903
Harry Smith	Ottawa Silver Seven	1906
Norm Smith	Detroit Red Wings	1936, 1937
Reginald "Hooley" Smith	Ottawa Senators	1927
	Montreal Maroons	1935
Rick Smith	Boston Bruins	1970
Sanford Smith	New York Rangers	1940
Sid Smith	Toronto Maple Leafs	1948, 1949, 1951
Steve Smith	Edmonton Oilers	1987, 1988, 1990
Tommy Smith	Ottawa Silver Seven	1906
	Quebec Bulldogs	1913
Rod Smylie	Toronto St Pats	1922
Doug Soetaert	Montreal Canadiens	1986
Art Somers	New York Rangers	1933
John Sorrell	Detroit Red Wings	1936, 1937
Bill Speer	Boston Bruins	1970
Charles D. Spittal	Ottawa Silver Seven	1903
Ted Stackhouse	Toronto St Pats	1922
Fred Stanfield	Boston Bruins	1970, 1972
Allan Stanley	Toronto Maple Leafs	1962, 1963, 1964, 1967

Barney Stanley	Vancouver Millionaires	1915
Wally Stanowski	Toronto Maple Leafs	1942, 1945, 1947, 1948
Paul Stanton	Pittsburgh Penguins	1991, 1992
Vic Stasiuk	Detroit Red Wings	1952, 1954, 1955
Pete Stemkowski	Toronto Maple Leafs	1967
Wayne Stephenson	Philadelphia Flyers	1975
Kevin Stevens	Pittsburgh Penguins	1991, 1992
Scott Stevens	New Jersey Devils	1995
Gaye Stewart	Toronto Maple Leafs	1942, 1947
Jack Stewart	Detroit Red Wings	1943, 1950
James Stewart	Montreal AAA	1893, 1894
Nels Stewart	Montreal Maroons	1926
Ron Stewart	Toronto Maple Leafs	1962, 1963, 1964
Dollard St. Laurent	Montreal Canadiens	1953, 1956, 1957, 1958
	Chicago Black Hawks	1961
Billy Strachan	Montreal Wanderers	1906, 1907
Billy Stuart	Toronto St Pats	1922
Bruce Stuart	Montreal Wanderers	1908
	Ottawa Senators	1909, 1911
Hod Stuart	Montreal Wanderers	1907
Gary Suter	Calgary Flames	1989
Brent Sutter	New York Islanders	1982, 1983
Duane Sutter	New York Islanders	1980, 1981, 1982, 1983
Petr Svoboda	Montreal Canadiens	1986
Darryl Sydor	Dallas Stars	1999
Peter Taglianetti	Pittsburgh Penguins	1991, 1992
Jean-Guy Talbot	Montreal Canadiens	1956, 1957, 1958, 1959, 1960, 1965, 1966
Steve Tambellini	New York Islanders	1980
Frank Tansey	Montreal Shamrocks	1899, 1900
Marc Tardif	Montreal Canadiens	1971, 1973
Bobby Taylor	Philadelphia Flyers	1974
Fred "Cyclone" Taylor	Ottawa Senators	1909
	Vancouver Millionaires	1915
Harry Taylor	Toronto Maple Leafs	1949
Tim Taylor	Detroit Red Wings	1997
Chris Terreri	New Jersey Devils	1995
Cecil "Tiny" Thompson	Boston Bruins	1929
Jim Thompson	Toronto Maple Leafs	1947, 1948, 1949, 1951
Paul Thompson	New York Rangers	1928
	Chicago Black Hawks	1934, 1938
Ray Timgren	Toronto Maple Leafs	1949, 1951
Esa Tikkanen	Edmonton Oilers	1985, 1987, 1988, 1990
	New York Rangers	1994
Rick Tocchet	Pittsburgh Penguins	1992
John Tonelli	New York Islanders	1980, 1981, 1982, 1983

Gilles Tremblay	Montreal Canadiens	1966, 1968
J.C. Tremblay	Montreal Canadiens	1965, 1966, 1968, 1969, 1971
Mario Tremblay	Montreal Canadiens	1976, 1977, 1978, 1979, 1986
Harry Trihey	Montreal Shamrocks	1899, 1900
Bryan Trottier	New York Islanders	1980, 1981, 1982, 1983
	Pittsburgh Penguins	1991, 1992
Dave Trottier	Montreal Maroons	1935
Lou Trudel	Chicago Black Hawks	1934, 1938
Roman Turek	Dallas Stars	1999
Bob Turner	Montreal Canadiens	1956
Rogie Vachon	Montreal Canadiens	1968, 1969, 1971
Carol Vadnais	Montreal Canadiens	1968
	Boston Bruins	1972
Ed Van Impe	Philadelphia Flyers	1974, 1975
Elmer "Moose" Vasco	Chicago Black Hawks	1961
Pat Verbeek	Dallas Stars	1999
Mike Vernon	Calgary Flames	1989
	Detroit Red Wings	1997
Georges Vezina	Montreal Canadiens	1916, 1924
Carl Voss	Chicago Black Hawks	1938
Frank Wall	Montreal Shamrocks	1899, 1900
Jack Walker	Toronto Blue Shirts	1914
	Seattle Metropolitans	1917
	Victoria Cougars	1925
Marty Walsh	Ottawa Senators	1909, 1911
Ryan Walter	Montreal Canadiens	1986
Mike Walton	Toronto Maple Leafs	1967
	Boston Bruins	1972
Rick Wamsley	Calgary Flames	1989
AC "Toad" Wand	Montreal AAA	1894
Aaron Ward	Detroit Red Wings	1997, 1998
Jimmy Ward	Montreal Maroons	1935
Eddie Wares	Detroit Red Wings	1943
Nick Wasnie	Montreal Canadiens	1930, 1931
Harry Watson	Detroit Red Wings	1943
	Toronto Maple Leafs	1947, 1948, 1949, 1951
Jimmy Watson	Philadelphia Flyers	1974, 1975
Joe Watson	Philadelphia Flyers	1974, 1975
Phil Watson	New York Rangers	1940
	Montreal Canadiens	1944
Ralph "Cooney" Weiland	Boston Bruins	1929, 1939
Jay Wells	New York Rangers	1994
Cy Wentworth	Montreal Maroons	1935
Ed Westfall	Boston Bruins	1970, 1972
Harry Westwick	Ottawa Silver Seven	1903, 1904, 1905, 1906
Kenny Wharram	Chicago Black Hawks	1961
Frank White	Ottawa Silver Seven	1905

143

Art Wiebe	Chicago Black Hawks	1938
Stanley Willett	Montreal Victorias	1896
Cully Wilson	Toronto Blue Shirts	1914
Johnny Wilson	Detroit Red Wings	1952, 1954, 1955
Murray Wilson	Montreal Canadiens	1973, 1976, 1978
Pete Wilson	Detroit Red Wings	1950
Eddie Wiseman	Boston Bruins	1941
Benny Woit	Detroit Red Wings	1952, 1954, 1955
Craig Wolanin	Colorado Avalanche	1996
Burke Wood	Winnipeg Victorias	1901, 1902
F.H. Wood	Ottawa Silver Seven	1903
Lorne "Gump" Worsley	Pittsburgh Penguins	1992
Stephane Yelle	Colorado Avalanche	1996
Doug Young	Detroit Red Wings	1936
Scott Young	Pittsburgh Penguins	1991
	Colorado Avalanche	1996
Wendell Young	Pittsburgh Penguins	1991, 1992
Steve Yzerman	Detroit Red Wings	1997, 1998
Valeri Zelepukin	New Jersey Devils	1995
Sergei Zubov	New York Rangers	1994
	Dallas Stars	1999

DATE DUE